PREVENTING VIOLENCE IN OUR SCHOOLS:

CLASSROOM ACTIVITIES AND STRATEGIES FOR TEACHERS AND COUNSELORS

Second Edition

Gerry Dunne, Ph.D.

JALMAR PRESS • CARSON, CALIFORNIA

Write to: Jalmar Press
P.O. Box 1185
Torrance, CA 90505

ISBN: 1-931061-25-4

Printed in the United States of America

DEDICATION...

To the students, teachers, and others who have been victimized by tragic violence in our schools and communities. May our awareness of your injuries and deaths serve as a jolt we won't forget to work together to keep the pain you suffered from happening to anyone else ever again.

MANY THANKS TO:

My husband, mentor and dearest friend, Dennis Alberson, LCSW, who consistently provided ideas and feedback for this curriculum that were right on target.

My colleagues and friends at Innerchoice Publishing and Jalmar Press: Susanna Palomares who assisted with research, ideas, materials and confidence that was contagious; Dave Cowan who turned my manuscript into a book; and Bradley Winch who demonstrated faith and patience.

My children, Rick, Dan and Lise Palomares, and friend Terri Akin, who gave me unlimited amounts of encouragement.

My Bible Study friends whose interest in this project jump-started me more than once to complete it.

Simon & Schuster Publishing Company for permission to summarize three stories from *The Moral Compass* by William Bennett.

AND SPECIAL ACKNOWLEDGMENT AND THANKS TO:

The William T. Grant Foundation and sixteen other foundations and corporations for providing the support for the development of *Safe Schools, Safe Students: A Guide to Violence Prevention Strategies* (Drug Strategies, Washington, DC, 1998), and to the board of directors, officers and consultants of Drug Strategies for developing this excellent guide. It provided numerous structural and content guidelines for the development of this curriculum. (To obtain a copy refer to "Great Resources," at the end of this book.)

CONTENTS...

INTRODUCTION

WHAT'S CAUSING THE VIOLENCE IN OUR SCHOOLS AND COMMUNITIES?

- *Lack of parental responsibility?*
- *Availability of weapons?*
- *Television?*
- *Unsafe conditions and lack of security in schools?*
- *Insufficient school counseling staffs?*
- *Domestic violence?*
- *Lack of religious faith?*
- *Coarsening of the culture?*
- *Movies?*
- *The internet?*

Certainly all of these factors in various combinations have contributed to violent tragedies in our schools and communities. However, the consistent ingredient that actually causes violence is inside violent individuals whether they are sane or insane. This ingredient is a combination of destructive emotions, urges and obsessions.

Violent behavior is set off by severe feelings like hatred, deep resentment, insignificance, alienation, fear, isolation, unworthiness, and jealousy coupled with urges to achieve revenge and notoriety. These are typically combined with mental activity focused solely on destructive ideas and plans without considering the full impact of contemplated actions or their consequences.

If we are going to prevent violence we must therefore be concerned with the inner experience of our students and attempt to understand how the conditions surrounding them are affecting that inner experience. Are we allowing them to

struggle to survive in unsafe and unfriendly physical and psychological environments at school where disrespectful behavior is tolerated? Or are we in the process of creating safe and supportive classrooms and a total school atmosphere that purposefully helps students learn to understand and get along with one another?

This curriculum is designed to significantly affect the inner life of students in grades four through twelve by offering a systematic series of learning experiences to be led by teachers and counselors. It is based on the belief that violence can be prevented when all students feel personally incorporated as valuable participants and have developed respect and caring for their fellow stakeholders in the learning community.

The activities in this curriculum primarily utilize the opinions, feelings, ideas, experiences and wisdom of the students themselves to promote understanding, build relationships, create compassion, and develop critical skills in communication, anger control, and conflict management. It has also been designed to provide students with the understanding and tools to build peace and harmony and to make conscious choices regarding significant human and media influences in their lives.

A high school principal whose school spent over $125,000 for security equipment and guards was asked by a reporter* whether a violent event like the one in

Littleton, Colorado could ever happen at his school. His instantaneous response was, "You bet!" Yes, we can spend money for security systems. But if we want safe schools, wouldn't we also be well advised to invest time, expertise and effort into enhancing the emotional and social development of our kids so that the safety of our schools doesn't have to be imposed, but rather comes from within?

---

*Kate Taylor, "The Puzzle of Prevention, First Part of a Three Part Series: More security but no guarantees--One of the nation's safest schools learns high-tech deterrents are only part of the solution to violence." Portland, Oregon: *The Oregonian*, May 2, 1999.

HOW THIS CURRICULUM ADDRESSES THE CAUSES OF VIOLENCE

One of the most difficult problems with gaining support for prevention programs is that when they work it can't be proven. Those who are dedicated to prevention do so by making educated assumptions and acting on faith. The key word is acting — doing something! Effort must be expended. Time must be taken. And teaching skills and developing knowledge of the subject must also be infused.

This curriculum offers ideas for ways to use that effort, time and expertise. It may not be possible to stop the unexpected, random assault of a psychotic individual but as numerous publications are telling us, public consciousness now sees student violence as predictable and preventable! The highly participative activities in this curriculum strategically offer carefully sequenced concepts and skills to build students' awareness and abilities to prevent violence.

Let's take a look at how the specific units of instruction can help you "act on faith" to work with the students to increase the safety and harmony of your school and community.

The first instructional unit in this curriculum is: **Communication Can Pave the Way to Understanding!**

Sheer isolation and alienation of students from other students can be easily seen on campuses, particularly secondary school sites, everywhere. In many cases the problem is even more severe than exclusion where students castigate, ridicule, torment, bully, and even physically assault each other. The unfortunate result is deep emotional injury which has led to retaliatory violence. *Communication Can Pave the Way to Understanding!* has been designed to counteract these conditions and behaviors.

It is essential that you lead all or most of the activities in this unit before proceeding to the following units in this curriculum because they provide a foundation for the more complex and challenging material in later units. As in all the subsequent units, these activities should be used in the order they are presented because the skills and concepts offered are built in a careful sequence. By focusing on communication, this unit develops interpersonal skills and provides enjoyable opportunities for students to know and appreciate each other. It is on this basis that the rest of the curriculum will be well received by the students.

The second instructional unit is: **Anger Can Be Managed!**

Anger is the fuel of violence. As we have witnessed throughout the ages it has prompted untold human misery and has been the driving force behind recent incidents of school violence. *Anger Can Be Managed!* is a core unit in this curriculum.

This unit has been designed to enlighten students about the normal and legitimate function of anger but also how easily it can cause destructive outcomes when out of control. The unit also emphasizes how anger can be controlled and used for positive purposes.

The third instructional unit is: **Influences Can be Chosen!**

While adult supervision is on the wane in most students' lives, they are simultaneously exposed to an increasing number of influences, including other people, particularly peers, and the media — movies, TV, news, and the internet. Although it is impossible to measure, it is generally held that these influences have contributed to violent acts committed by students. *Influences Can Be Chosen!* increases student's awareness of these influences in their lives.

This unit enables students to evaluate the influences in their lives. It also assists them to discriminate between the constructive and destructive ones they encounter daily so they can choose who and what will influence them and how.

The fourth instructional unit is: **Violence Can Be Stopped Before It Starts!**

Many times serious violence occurs as an outgrowth or escalation of a conflict that could have been avoided or resolved before it got out of hand. *Violence Can Be Stopped Before It Starts!* is a critically important unit in this curriculum offering a carefully sequenced series of activities with concepts and skills that build on one another.

The activities in this unit offer key concepts and understandings about conflict and skills for managing it with a special emphasis on how to defuse potentially violent situations and people.

The fifth instructional unit is: **Peace and Harmony Can Be Created!**

One of the best ways to prevent violence is to focus on more than simply preventing it. Instead, social environments can be established that not only accept but honor human differences including race, culture, faith, economic level, interests, talents, gender, age, opinions, etc. In such an environment violence is very unlikely to germinate or develop. *Peace and Harmony Can Be Created!* has been designed to help students work together to establish and maintain such a community.

This unit focuses on developing the understandings, qualities and skills needed to create a cooperative, productive social environment by continuing to build students' interpersonal abilities, tolerance and appreciation of others, feelings of self worth, and a strong sense of belonging.

SINGULAR POSITIVE ACTIONS FOR TEACHERS AND COUNSELORS

- Smile at each student at least once a day especially when they aren't smiling!

- Greet students individually as often as you can; say their names!

- Get to know your students--their likes, dislikes, talents, and special interests!

- Pat your students on the back. Show them nonverbally you care for them!

- Let students see who you are. Don't be afraid to tell them about yourself!

- Go to student events and have a great time!

- Ask students about the things they are wearing like jewelry or items of clothing!

- Set students up for success!

- Encourage questions about assignments and material they find puzzling!

- Point out the value of learning from errors and mistakes!

- Encourage creativity and ways to have fun when fulfilling assignments!

- Acknowledge effort!

- Ask students for feedback and suggestions!

- When problems arise call students on the telephone asking them to explain what happened from their point of view and how they are feeling.

- Teach empathy!

- Focus on things students do right! Acknowledge academic competence!

- Look for the positive even when there seems to be no positive!

- Laugh with your students. Have fun!

- Listen, listen, and listen some more!

These ideas were inspired in part by Richard L. Curwin and Allen N. Mendler in their excellent book: *As Tough as Necessary: Countering Violence, Aggression, and Hostility in our Schools,* Alexandria, Virginia: Association for Supervision and Curriculum Development, 1997. You can obtain this book by calling ASCD at (800) 933-2723 or (703) 549-9110.

THE CIRCLE SESSION: CONNECTING AND RECONNECTING

Civilization began when human beings sat down in a circle to share their experiences, feelings and ideas.

Author unknown.

With any age group and under the right conditions the circle session can accomplish more than any other process model to help people understand and appreciate themselves and each other while they practice pro-social communication skills and examine the human condition. When introduced and conducted skillfully, and when participants honor the ground rules, the circle session is a powerful vehicle that fosters self respect within individuals and a sense of community of co-learners within a group. It provides an opportunity for participants to personally and meaningfully connect with each other and to reconnect again and again as they continue to experience more circle sessions.

The circle session model is simple and easy to use, but does require that you follow very specific steps and ground rules. The results are well worth the effort. Let's discuss all of these beginning with preparations for setting up circle sessions:

MAKING PREPARATIONS

Group Size and Composition:

Circle sessions are a time for focusing on individuals' contributions in an unhurried fashion. For this reason, each circle session group needs to be kept relatively small — four to six usually works best. More than twelve in a group becomes unwieldy. Fourth through twelfth graders are capable of extensive verbalization and will be more inclined to participate if their group size is small.

Each group should be as heterogeneous as possible with respect to gender, ability, interests, and culture. Sometimes there will be a group in which all of the students are particularly reticent to speak. In these instances bring in an expressive student or two who will get things going. Sometimes it is necessary for practical reasons to change membership of a group. Once established, however, it is advisable to keep group membership as stable as possible.

Length and Location of Circle Sessions:

Most circle sessions last approximately 15 to 20 minutes, sometimes a little longer. At first many students tend to be reluctant to express themselves because they don't know yet that the circle is a safe place. Consequently your first sessions may not last more than a few minutes. Experience has shown that students become comfortable and motivated to speak with continued exposure to the process, however, and as they participate more the sessions last longer.

At the elementary level, circle sessions may be carried out anytime during the day. At middle and high school levels, circle sessions may be conducted at any time during a typical 50 minute class period. Starting circle sessions at the beginning of the period allows additional time in case students become deeply involved in the topic. If you start circles late in the period, make sure they are aware of their responsibility to be concise.

Circle sessions may be carried out wherever there is room for students to sit in a circle and experience few or no distractions. Most teachers and counselors prefer to have students sit on chairs or at their desks which have been turned into a circle rather than sitting on the floor because they seem less prone to invade one another's space while seated in chairs or at their desks. Sometimes sessions are conducted outdoors as long as distractions are minimized.

How to Get Started:

The second activity in the first unit, "Introducing the Process," provides directions for introducing the circle session to the students beginning with forming groups and a dyad activity allowing students to speak briefly on a one-to-one basis with some of the members of their group. This helps "break the ice" before they experience their first circle session.

Here are two other ways to initiate the circle session process:

Establish inner and outer circles. Conduct a circle session with six to eight students in an inner circle as the rest of the class observes and listens. After the session, these students trade places with a like number in the outer circle. This process continues until all students have had a chance to participate in the inner circle while the others watch and listen, perhaps spread over two consecutive days. If you ask the students in the outer circle to participate in the summary discussion at the end of each session it will make the process more interesting for them. After you have completed this process, your class is ready to participate in simultaneous circle sessions. For their first few sessions assist leaders by "walking them through" the process step-by-step. Later, the students will understand and be comfortable with the leadership role. (See "Training Student Leaders," presented later in this section.)

Gradually establish circle session groups. This is a favorite for many teachers and counselors. After making your presentation to the class about circle sessions, select a small number of particularly cooperative, well-liked and expressive students and hold a session with them while the rest of the class attends to other silent activities. These could include: writing in journals on the same topic, completing an assignment, studying, conducting research in the library or computer lab, or even listening to what is being said in the circle session. (It helps if you have an aide, parent volunteer, or other staff member in the classroom to attend to the needs of the students who are not circle members.) This approach usually initiates keen interest in the students who did not participate in the circle session and questions about when they will get their chance.

Continue to meet with this group in this manner, formally training them to lead circle sessions themselves. (Refer to "How to Train Student Leaders") When these students feel ready, organize the class into groups with these students as their leaders.

An even more gradual approach would be to start a second group after the first group has experienced several sessions and repeat the process with them while the first group continues to meet by themselves with student leaders. The logical choice of members for the second group would be those students who expressed an interest in becoming a part of the process. After both established groups are ready they may be divided among the rest of the class and simultaneous circle sessions may be begun with these students in control of leadership and training others to be leaders as well. At this point you may circulate while simultaneous circle sessions are occurring or sit down with a group as a participant while a student leads.

The key to initiating and carrying out circle sessions is to select a process that will work for you. Set yourself up for success and everyone will benefit!

PROCEDURES FOR LEADING A CIRCLE SESSION

This section is a thorough guide for conducting circle sessions. It covers key points to keep in mind and answers questions which are likely to arise. Please remember that these guidelines are presented to assist you, not to be restrictive. Follow them and trust your own leadership style at the same time.

Here is the same chart recommended for presentation to the students when you introduce the process to them. Be sure to read all of the procedural directions and recommendations in this section to yourself to become prepared to lead circle sessions. When you present this information to the students cover the procedures briefly concentrating primarily on discussing the ground rules. (The chart and suggestions for how to present each ground rule are given shortly.)

Circle Session Procedures

1. Set up the circle and the tone. (1 - 2 minutes)

2. Review the Ground Rules. (1 - 2 minutes)

3. Introduce the topic. (1 - 2 minutes)

4. Each member may speak to the topic. (5 - 15 minutes)

5. Optional: Review what was said. (3 - 5 minutes)

6. Summary discussion. (2 - 8 minutes)

7. Close the circle. (Less than one minute.)

Let's discuss each one of these steps:

1. Set up the circle and the tone. (1 - 2 minutes)

As you sit down with the students in the circle, remember that you are not teaching a lesson or facilitating a free-flowing encounter or therapy group. You are leading a carefully structured educational activity in which the participants are the source of information. First, make sure the circle is round so that each person can see everyone else. Establish a positive atmosphere. In a calm manner address each student by name with a greeting using eye contact and conveying warmth and respect. An attitude of seriousness blended with enthusiasm will let the students know that the circle session is an important learning experience — an activity that can be interesting and important to them.

2. Review the Ground Rules. (1 - 2 minutes)

At the beginning of the first few circle sessions and at appropriate intervals go over the rules for the circle session. They are:

Ground Rules for the Circle Session

1. Bring yourself to the circle and nothing else.

2. Everyone gets a turn to share including the leader.

3. You can skip your turn if you wish.

4. Listen to the person who is speaking.

5. The time is shared equally.

6. Stay in your own space.

7. There are no interruptions, probing, put-downs, or gossip.

8. What is discussed in the circle stays in the circle.

Briefly explain these rules to the students as follows:

- **Bring yourself to the circle and nothing else.** *Books, paper, pencils, or anything else are not necessary to bring to the circle. They cause distractions. All you need to bring to the circle is yourself because you have within you everything you need to participate.*

- **Everyone gets a turn to share including the leader.** *Everyone is equally important and is given respect in the circle session so everyone gets one turn to speak to the topic.*

- **You can skip your turn if you wish.** *If you choose to participate by listening only, that's okay. You will not be forced to say anything if you prefer not to. The leader might not be sure if you want to say something or not and may invite you to take a turn, but if you don't want to speak just let the leader know.*

- **Listen to the person who is speaking.** *While one person is taking a turn to speak to the topic the rest of us will remain completely silent and just listen.*

- **The time is shared equally.** *This rule means that we should each take about a minute or a little longer when it is our turn to speak to the topic. Be sure not to go over two minutes. If one person speaks for too long the time gets eaten up and others may not have a chance.*

- **Stay in your own space.** *This means that each one of us will behave in a mature manner and not bother someone else physically during the session.*

- **There are no interruptions, probing, put-downs, or gossip.** *These are four things to avoid. Just listen silently when someone is speaking. Don't butt in and don't ask questions. If a question comes to your mind stop yourself from asking it during the session. Instead, wait till it's over to ask the person your question. Putting someone down verbally or nonverbally is completely unacceptable. I will not allow anyone to do it to you and I won't allow you to do it to anyone else. Gossip is also unacceptable. If you are taking a turn to speak to a topic and you are telling about something that happened that involved someone else and you know it would embarrass them if they knew you told who they were, don't say their name. Just say 'someone I know.'*

- **What is discussed in the circle stays in the circle.** *This means that we all agree not to repeat what we heard someone say in a circle session to anyone else later. What you tell about still belongs to you. It's not okay for someone in the circle to take it away and spread it around. This works both ways and we will all be responsible for honoring this ground rule.*

3. Introduce the topic. (1 - 2 minutes)

This four-step process works well for introducing the topic:

- State the topic.

- Elaborate on the topic in your own words adding clarifying statements that will help the students understand it; answer any questions they may have.

- Restate the topic.

- Suggest the students take a few moments to silently think about it, closing their eyes if they wish. Tell them you will know they are ready to begin discussing the topic when they are looking at you.

Prior to leading the session contemplate the topic and decide on a response you would like to make. Sometimes it is helpful to the students if you take your turn first, but don't do this every time. If the responses students give later are off the topic, repeat it again to help them get back on track.

Note: One of the best ways to ensure a successful circle session with full participation and expression from students is to post the topic for the session on the chalkboard — before it occurs — even a day or two ahead. This gives them time to think about it and prepare their responses.

4. Each member may speak to the topic. (5 - 15 minutes)

When the students are looking at you expectantly, ask, "Who is ready?" or "Who would like to go first?" Then select a student who indicates readiness to speak to the topic and give him or her the nod. Never "call on" someone who has not indicated he or she wishes to speak. Many students wish to speak but prefer to be invited to take a turn, however. If a student looks ready but hasn't said so, offer an invitation by asking, *Victor, would you like to take a turn?* (Accept all refusals with complete acceptance.)

During this phase of the session enforce the ground rules by reminding offenders politely but firmly of the rule they are breaking. If repeated offenses occur talk to the offenders on a one-to-one basis after the session soliciting their help to make the circle session more pleasant and enjoyable. Only on very rare and extreme occasions should you ever ask a student to leave the circle. It is better to exclude students who severely and repeatedly break the ground rules from future sessions, explaining to them that you would be pleased to readmit them when they promise to demonstrate that they are mature enough to honor the ground rules.

The most important thing to remember is this: The purpose of the circle session is to give the students an opportunity to express themselves and be accepted for the experiences, feelings and thoughts they share. Avoid taking the action away from them. They are the stars!

5. Optional: Review what was said. (3 - 5 minutes)

The review serves as a listening check and strengthener. It reinforces students for listening well and allows students who may have not chosen to speak to the topic the chance to speak in the session by telling another student what he or she heard the other student say. It also demonstrates to students who spoke to the topic that they were heard and are therefore important.

To initiate a review go first. Select a student and briefly paraphrase what you heard him or her say: *Karen, you told about how much you enjoy it when your family goes camping at Lake Tapawingo. The lake is a favorite place for you because it's beautiful and peaceful. There's also a lot of kids your*

age there who you make friends with each year. Did I hear you right? Listen to the student's response including any possible corrections and then ask, *Who else would like to tell another person what you heard him or her say?* Call on the student and continue in this manner until everyone who took a turn to speak to the topic has been reviewed to.

Note: This is not a time to give one's opinion about what someone said or to add a story of one's own by saying something like: *I can relate to what you said because I have a lake I like to go to also. It's...(blah, blah, blah).* It is also very important that the reviewer speak directly to the person he or she is reviewing, using the person's name and the pronoun, "you," not "he," or "she." If a student begins to review to another student and says, "She said that...," intervene as promptly and respectfully as possible and say to the reviewer: *Talk to Betty. Say 'you' to her.* The effect on the person reviewed to is much more positive when spoken to instead of being spoken about.

Another note: Remember, the review is optional and is most effective when used intermittently, not as a part of every circle.

6. Summary discussion. (2 - 8 minutes)

The summary discussion is not optional. It is the cognitive portion of the circle session, the point at which the students find meaning in what they have shared. It is a very important part of the session and should never be dispensed with. During this phase ask thought-provoking questions to stimulate higher-level thinking and open, free discussion. Each circle session description in this curriculum offers at least two questions to spark this discussion but you may use others of your own that are more appropriate to the level of understanding in your group.

It is important not to confuse the summary discussion (Step 6) with the Review (Step 5). They are very different from each other. The summary serves as a necessary culmination to each circle session by allowing the students to clarify the key concepts and conclusions they have gained.

7. Close the circle. (Less than one minute.)

Always bring formal closure to each circle session. The ideal time is when the summary discussion reaches a natural ending. Sincerely thank the students for being part of the session. (Don't thank specific ones for speaking as doing so might convey the impression that speaking is more appreciated than listening.) Then close the circle by saying: "The circle session is now closed," or "Okay, that ends our session."

TRAINING STUDENT LEADERS

A basic assumption of this program is that all students of normal intelligence have leadership potential. The best time to energize this ability is in childhood and the optimum time for maintaining the skills is during adolescence. Students in countless classrooms effectively lead their own circle sessions.

Leadership training for the circle session can be provided in several stages. In the first stage of training, the student observes you and begins to acquire the skills of leadership through observation and later by simple imitation. Many students are ready to repeat your actions even after one observation.

Another stage of leadership training occurs when you divide your class into groups for simultaneous circle sessions and ask the groups to select a leader. (Before doing this write the topic and the discussion questions on the board for reference later.) At this point it may work best to ask the students who would like to lead to volunteer for the role. (If no one volunteers in a group suggest they choose someone they believe is capable of handling the challenge. Most students are pleased to be chosen.) Assure the leaders that you will help them.

Assist the leaders by "walking them through" the process. This is done by announcing to the groups, *Leaders, make sure your group is sitting in a circle and that everyone is comfortable. Take a minute to greet each person.* (Wait one minute as the leaders do this.) *The topic is: ('A Time When I Was Pleasantly Surprised').* (Elaborate on the topic yourself by saying the suggested elaboration in the circle session description in your own words. *Think about it for a few moments silently and when you look at your leader he or she will know you are ready to start.* (Provide one half minute for silent thinking.) *Leaders, now ask who would like to begin. I am going to give you about five minutes so that everyone in your group can take a turn to speak to the topic. If you finish before that you may ask the circle members to tell each other what they heard each other say. If all of the groups aren't finished I'll give you more time. Begin.* (Allow at least five minutes.) *Now, let's discuss the (two) summary questions. Allow all of the members of your group to respond to the first one who wish to and then do the same for the second one. You will have three more minutes for this summary discussion.* (Allow three minutes.) *The time is up. Leaders, close your circle sessions.* (Allow about 15 seconds.)

A good follow-up to this process is to ask each circle session group to take one more minute to tell their leader what he or she did as leader that was skillful and helpful. Then, as the class listens, ask each group how their session went. React to their remarks by emphasizing the positives, particularly skills demonstrated by the leader.

A third stage of leadership training may occur for students who indicate their interest in becoming leaders after they have participated in several circle sessions led by you. Work with one student at a time. Give him or her a copy of the circle session description in this curriculum that you would like him or her to lead for prior study. Then sit down next to the student in the session and announce to the group that you are the trainer but the student is the leader and you will participate just like them. Before turning the session over to the student leader, add one more thing — a new ground rule stating that the students are expected to respect the student's leadership position. They should not prompt or criticize him or her during the session.

Before leaving the circle thank the student leader and ask the students to tell him or her what they appreciated about the way he or she conducted the session. Next, ask if there are any suggestions. Let the student leader call on anyone who wishes to make a comment. Finally, tell the students the topic you have in mind for the next session and ask for a volunteer to lead it. Select a student who you are sure will be successful. (Be sure to select students from diverse backgrounds.) Continue this process until all who wish to conduct circles are competent enough to lead them independently.

TIPS FOR LEADING THE ACTIVITIES IN THIS CURRICULUM

William Glasser stated that we learn:
10% of what we read,
20% of what we hear,
30% of what we see,
50% of what we both see and hear,
70% of what is discussed with others,
80% of what we experience personally, and
95% of what we teach to someone else!

This curriculum offers learning experiences including circle sessions and "Introductory, " "Fundamental," and "Culminating," activities to students in all of the categories named above by Dr. Glasser. The vast majority include interaction and discussion wherein students are the primary educational resource themselves.

Let's discuss some of the types of activities besides circle sessions that are offered and tips for leading them:

Discussions:

Discussions are of critical importance in this curriculum. Almost every activity involves class discussion at its close to bring meaning to the experience and to assist students to draw important conclusions. Sometimes the discussions are better timed when they occur during the activity. In all cases sample discussion questions are offered and for some discussions where specific answers are vital these are provided.

A tip for conducting good discussions: after you have asked a question, always wait longer than you think you should have to to hear responses. It takes time for the students to think and to formulate their thoughts into words. A good rule of thumb is to wait four seconds before responding to the question yourself or calling on a student who seems to have something to say.

Be sure to allow every student who wishes to respond to a question the chance to do so. Without being rigid, ask students who introduce peripheral issues to bring them up again when the main discussion is over or at another time. Digressions can impair the effectiveness of guided discussions. However, the other thoughts students introduce are often worth discussion as well so do return to them.

Task Groups:

A number of the activities in this curriculum call for dividing the class into task groups. These may be established circle session groups, cooperative learning groups, or groups assembled for this onetime, ad hoc purpose. Four students per group is usually the best number. It generally helps for each group to assign roles to the members including a leader, recorder, process consultant, encourager, liaison to the teacher/counselor, etc.

As task groups work circulate and visit each one to serve as a consultant when needed. Offer suggestions, if necessary, as well as encouragement, support and praise. If a group has a "detractor" that you spot, ask him or her to come and speak with you in private. Be positive. Let the student know you are counting on him or her to contribute to the group's efforts and so are the members of the group.

Scenarios, dramatizations and role plays

Some scenarios in the curriculum are offered only as reading and discussion material. Other scenarios are read, acted out in impromptu dramatizations and then discussed. Other activities offer suggestions for dramatizations (where students play the parts of someone other than themselves) and role plays (where students play the parts of themselves in a given situation).

Besides being very dynamic, acting experiences in the classroom promote direct, experiential learning. Dramatizations may involve planning, rehearsing, and performing, and may call for a student director and/or narrator. Role playing is usually more spontaneous and unfolds in a situation that simulates reality. It is frequently used as a problem solving technique in which alternative actions are tested and evaluated.

Brainstorming

Brainstorming is a very valuable way to promote individual creativity and group cohesiveness at the same time. A number of the activities in this curriculum call for brainstorming in which students are asked to spontaneously generate ideas or reactions which are recorded (or charted) and used in some way as the activity progresses.

The most important thing to remember about brainstorming is that the generation of ideas and the evaluation of those ideas are two separate processes. Thanks to this distinction, individuals may contribute their ideas spontaneously without fear of criticism.

Brainstorming includes the following basic steps:

- The challenge (task or problem) is defined.

- The students name and describe all the ideas or reactions they can think of without evaluating any of them. These are recorded as they are given.

- The brainstorming is ended.

- Then and only then are the ideas analyzed or evaluated.

- A choice or decision is made, if appropriate.

Team Teaching Performed by Students

Some of the most robust activities in this curriculum suggest that the students take the role of team teachers. (It is also suggested that teachers/counselors of grades four through six may prefer to teach the information offered in these activity descriptions to their classes themselves.) Older students are generally capable of meeting this challenge themselves. In fact, most relish it and do a very good job.

These activities entail providing information sheets to task groups who read and discuss the material together and plan how to teach it as a team to their peers.

Teachers/counselors serve as consultants to the groups during the planning stages. The students are encouraged to be creative with visual aids, examples, dramatizations, related music or poetry, quotations from related research found in the library or on the internet, etc. As the students make their presentations the teacher/counselor models listening, attentiveness and appreciation. In each case applause and discussion follows the presentation given by the students.

HOW TO USE THIS BOOK MOST EFFECTIVELY

Please don't focus on violence. This curriculum emphasizes strategies for creating peace and stopping violence before it starts. Don't allow students to describe violent scenes in detail or to act them out in dramatizations or role plays. These have been shown to be very ineffective in violence prevention programs. To repeat the main point: emphasis in discussion and demonstration should always be placed on ways to respond to violent or potentially violent situations in order to prevent or defuse them.

Present the units and the activities within each unit in the order given. *Preventing Violence in Our Schools* is a developmental and sequential program of activities and circle sessions. In order for the program to have the impact intended, we strongly urge you to present the units in the order given. Also, the concepts within each unit build on one another and the activities in each unit are presented in the recommended order. By following this order, you will ensure the greatest benefit and skill development to your students.

Feel free to adjust and modify activities to suit the ages, ability levels, cultural/ethnic backgrounds, and interests of your students. You know best how to maximize the appropriateness and impact of each activity.

Please don't try to repeat the words offered in the activity descriptions verbatim. Throughout this curriculum directions are frequently given for ways to speak to the students with exact wordings offered. Because the content of the activities is often subtle and sensitive, this is done to convey "flavor" to you as you make preparations. It is not intended that you attempt to repeat these words verbatim or read them to the class. In fact, reading them is likely to be ineffective and "turn off" the students. Rather, the activities will work best when you give directions and make statements in your own words so that your class will recognize that they have come from you.

Please don't allow circle session participants to break the ground rules during circle sessions. Surprisingly, the rule about not asking questions to someone who is responding to the topic is particularly important. The natural tendency in conversations is to ask questions whenever one comes to mind so abiding by this rule can be difficult. Counselors are the ones who might have the most difficulty. This is because counselors are trained to ask questions in individual and group counseling situations. But the circle session is different — it's an educational classroom experience, not group counseling or "therapy" of any kind. The fact is that when a circle session is in progress and individuals are taking their turns to speak to the topic, questions asked to them by the other participants will derail them. This seriously undermines the effectiveness the session.

Here's what to do: Follow the rule about no probing yourself. Model silent listening as a student speaks with no questions of your own until the session has been closed. Second, enforce the rule by politely, but firmly, reminding students who break it that they should save their questions until afterward. An added benefit of saving questions until after the session is the interaction that occurs between students who otherwise may not have been inclined to speak with one another. This initiates and builds relationships!

Counselors: Invite others to do the activities with you. If no one else is willing to become involved, leading some of the activities in some classrooms as you are able is better than nothing. There's no way you can do it alone even if you completely exhaust yourself — that is, if you really want significantly positive school-wide outcomes. (Worst case scenario: a counselor tries to reach all classrooms and even tells teachers to go get a cup of coffee while the counselor leads activities in their classrooms. At the very least teachers should be asked to observe.) The fact is

that since this is a classroom educational program, the instructional units and activities have been designed for teachers to lead with their students. There is no better way for school-wide improvement of the social environment to occur.

Here's a broader vision for your role: empower teachers by training them and through support and encouragement as they render this program. First, demonstrate to groups of teachers how to lead the activities. Visit classrooms, not to lead activities, but to observe teachers as they lead them and meet with each teacher afterward to give positive feedback and encouragement to persevere. Hold occasional meetings with teachers in groups to troubleshoot and share success stories. Call Jalmar Press, (310) 816-3085 if you want help. We conduct specially designed consultations and training sessions to empower counselors to empower teachers and involve parents as well.

COMMUNICATION CAN PAVE THE WAY TO UNDERSTANDING!

OVERVIEW . . .

The first goal of this introductory unit is to begin to create a sense of community among the students in your class or counseling group where each student belongs and is valued. This strong "team consciousness" facilitates readiness within students to keep learning together. It is achieved when they consistently interact with each other in safe and enjoyable, yet challenging ways to build social skills they know are useful.

The second goal is to build those skills by assisting students to understand the elements of effective communication and how to interact with others in a variety of situations. These interpersonal skills will serve them as they embark on the activities in the rest of this curriculum and beyond. They include speaking clearly, listening to words and more than words, using effective body language, avoiding actions that thwart communication, and employing strategies that pave the way to understanding and developing positive relationships.

Through a variety of active processes, this instructional unit has been designed to provide learning experiences that teach the following information or "understandings" about communication:

- Good introductions can facilitate the creation of good relationships.

- Everyone can improve their speaking and listening skills through practice.

- When speaking, come to the point, be as clear as possible, and consider how you can help your listener understand your message.

- Perhaps the most effective listening strategy is to stop talking or thinking about what you want to say; rather, focus entirely on the speaker to hear what he or she is saying.

- When listening, mentally tape record what someone is saying. It often helps to check to find out if you heard a speaker correctly.

- Asking questions of speakers can be helpful if you don't understand them, but questions can divert them from what they originally wanted to say. Too many questions can seem like an interrogation and put speakers on the defensive.

- Our nonverbal communications or "body language" are constantly sending positive and/or negative messages to others. These include eye contact or the lack of it, facial expressions, turning the body toward and away or moving toward or away from another person, showing open and closed body postures, and using assorted gestures.

- Many nonverbal modes of communication have different meanings in different cultures.

- Eight behaviors that typically retard or stop communication are:

  - Interrupting
  - Dominating
  - Judging
  - Probing
  - Giving Unasked-for Advice
  - Misinterpreting
  - Accusing/Contradicting/Criticizing
  - Putting Down/Name-calling/ Ridiculing

- Many times the words and phrases people use do not reflect their real message or needs. This is most apt to happen when they are experiencing uncomfortable emotions like embarrassment, insignificance, anger, fear, jealousy, insecurity or guilt.

- When people say one thing and actually mean something else listeners who wish to be helpful can "listen with the third ear" to try to determine the real message. When listeners aren't sure they can ask questions in a kind and sincere manner.

- When listeners "listen with the third ear" and respond calmly to the feelings and needs of speakers, as opposed to their words, they can assist speakers to feel better and defuse potentially difficult situations.

- Self talk is constant and powerful. It can be helpful or hurtful. People can train themselves to use positive self talk.

An excellent source for additional activities fostering interpersonal communication: *Impact! A Self-Esteem Based Skill Development Program for Secondary Students* by Gerry Dunne, Ph.D., Dianne Schilling, M.S. and David Cowan, M.A., Carson, California: Innerchoice Publishing Company, 1990. Phone: (310) 816-3085.

INTRODUCING OURSELVES!
Three Introductory Activities

Note to teachers and counselors:

Friendly introductions are very beneficial and necessary. Be sure to conduct at least one of the three introduction activities offered here.

Activity One —

Description:

Students pair up and form dyads, taking turns introducing themselves to their partners. This includes their name, how they got their name, and something interesting about them that no one would know unless they told about it. Next students introduce their partners to the class.

Objectives:

Students will:

— get to know each other, and learn interesting information about each other, in enjoyable ways.

— create a foundation for building relationships and practicing interpersonal skills.

Time needed:

20 to 40 minutes

Materials needed:

Prepare the following on the chalkboard or chart before class:

Introductions Today! Tell your partner:

1. *Your name.*

2. *How you got your name.*

3. *Something interesting about you that people would never know unless you told them.*

Directions:

1. Introduce the activity: *Let's get to know each other and use our communication skills at the same time. You will have a partner for this exercise. You will listen as your partner introduces him or herself to you and then you will introduce yourself to your partner. After that you will introduce your partner to the class. No note-taking. Just see how well you listen and remember.*

2. Help the students pair up and form dyads. This is done by turning their desks or chairs so they are facing each other. (If you have an odd number of students be the partner to the remaining student.) Ask them to take five seconds to decide who will be A and who will be B. Then ask to see the hands of the A's and the B's. When everyone has responded point to the directions on the chalkboard, or chart, and explain: *The A's will speak first for two minutes. Tell your partner your name and how you got it. For example, you may have been named after a family member or someone famous, or maybe your parents just liked the name so they gave it to you. Last, think of something unusual or interesting about yourself that people wouldn't know unless you told them. Tell something that wouldn't embarrass you to talk about or for another person to hear.*

3. After two minutes direct the B's to take their turns to speak to the A's to the same topic.

4. Give the students two additional minutes to make sure they correctly remember their facts about each other before introductions are made to the class.

5. Facilitate the introductions. Make it formal, but fun.! Ask each pair to come to the front of the class and introduce each other. Lead an applause after each introduction.

Activity Two —

Description:

A name tag for a fellow student is placed on the back of each student. Then students mingle and ask questions of one another to try to determine whose name tag they have. When they have found the proper "owner" of these name tags, they give them to those individuals. Then they sit down and help from the sidelines.

Objective:

Students will:

— get to know each other, and learn interesting information about each other, in enjoyable ways.

— create a foundation for building relationships and practicing interpersonal skills.

Time needed:

10 to 20 minutes

Materials needed:

One name tag for each student with his/her name written on it in big letters. Prepare the following on the chalkboard or chart before class:

Find the "Owner" of the Name Tag You Have on Your Back.

Here are the rules:

1. *Ask questions of other students that can only be answered "yes" or "no."*

2. *When you think you know whose name tag you have, ask the person directly. If correct, give him or her the name tag and sit down.*

3. *When someone has your name tag and finds you, stick your name tag on yourself where it can be easily seen.*

4. *Once you are seated, help from the sidelines by answering questions and giving clues.*

Directions:

1. As the students enter the classroom, greet them and stick a name tag of a fellow student on each one's back.

2. Before the activity begins, give students some sample "Do I" and "Am I" questions (e.g., Am I a girl? Am I tall? Do I play a sport? Do I have brown hair?).

3. Point out the rules of the activity on the chalkboard or chart and let them begin right away to find the "owners" of their name tags.

4. When everyone has been seated, tell the students about some of the interesting and/or funny things you observed as they engaged in the activity. Ask: *Did anyone else see something interesting or funny or did something funny happen to you?* Let every student who wishes to respond have a chance to do so. Enjoy reflecting on the experience together and laughing about the amusing things that may have happened.

5. Acknowledge the students for their participation and for making the activity so much fun.

Activity Three —

Description:

Students are provided a "Bingo Card" with slots for characteristics of classmates. Then they circulate to see how many fellow students they can find with those characteristics and obtain signatures for their cards. Students with completed cards sit down and help from the sidelines.

Objective:

Students will:

— get to know each other, and learn interesting information about each other, in enjoyable ways.

— create a foundation for building relationships and practicing interpersonal skills.

Time needed:

10 to 20 minutes

Materials needed:

One copy of the "Getting to Know You Better Bingo" form for each student (See next page). Prepare the following on the chalkboard or chart before class:

Play "Getting to Know You Better Bingo!"

Here are the rules:

1. *Talk to each other to find out who has the characteristics on your Bingo form.*

2. *Have people sign their name in the box where their characteristic is written.*

3. *Another person may sign your form only once.*

4. *Sit down when your form is filled in. Once you are seated help from the sidelines by giving clues.*

Directions:

1. As the students enter the classroom greet them and hand each one a "Getting to Know You Better Bingo" form. Direct their attention to the posted rules for the activity and encourage them to begin right away to try to fill up their forms with signatures.

2. When everyone is seated, engage the class in discussion regarding who had which particular characteristics. For example, ask: *Who has been to a national park within the last two years?* (As names are stated, ask the students named to tell the class which parks they visited and when, etc.) *Who is left-handed?* (As names are stated, ask if any of them are ambidextrous, etc.)

3. Acknowledge the students for their energetic involvement which made the activity enjoyable.

Getting to Know You Better Bingo!

Has been to a national park within the last two years.	Is left-handed.	Collects something.
Was born in the summer.	Likes to play baseball.	Has an older sister.
Likes to "surf the web."	Has a part-time or temporary job.	Knows how to ride a horse.
Likes to sing.	Has a younger brother.	Likes to cook.
Can juggle.	Has seen a skunk in the wild.	Can lift one eyebrow without lifting the other.

INTRODUCING THE PROCESS
Dyads, Teacher/Counselor Presentation and Discussion
An Introductory Activity

The purpose of this activity is to prepare students to participate in circle sessions. Part One is an "ice breaker" enabling students to begin speaking to each other on a one-to-one basis and getting to know each other better. This helps them feel more comfortable and willing to participate in the upcoming circle session. Part Two explains to the students the purpose of circle sessions and how they operate.

Description:

Part One: After a brief descriptive overview of this program, the students are put into small groups of six members from which they form dyads. Topics are given to the dyads with partners taking one minute turns to speak and listen to one another. Dyad partners are changed twice so each student will have a turn to personally speak and listen to three other members of his/her group. A brief class discussion about the dyad experience follows.

Part Two: The teacher/counselor explains the purposes and procedures of a circle session as a prelude to the first circle session the class will experience.

Objectives:

Students will:

— speak and listen to three different partners in dyad discussions.

— participate in a class discussion regarding their reactions to speaking and listening to each other in dyads.

— listen to a presentation on the purposes and procedures of a circle session.

— participate in a circle session using speaking and listening skills.

Time needed:

60 to 80 minutes, but the activity may be split into separate sessions if necessary.

Materials needed:

Charts One through Four. These should be posted in the classroom for the duration of the program. The charts are:

Chart One:

Topics for Today:

"A Favorite Musical Group or Song of Mine"
"A Favorite Game or Sport of Mine"
"A Favorite Book or Story of Mine"
"A Favorite Movie or TV Show of Mine"
"A Favorite Famous Person of Mine"
"A Favorite Nonfamous Person of Mine"
"A Favorite Place of Mine"
"A Time When I Was Pleasantly Surprised"

Chart Two:

Why Have a Session in a Circle?

- A circle has no front, middle or back.
- We're all side-by-side and equal to each other.
- We can all see each other.
- Circle membership is small to allow for good participation.

What is the circle session for?

To discuss:
    Experiences
    Feelings
    Thoughts
    Conclusions

Chart Three:

Circle Session Procedures

1. Set up the circle and the tone.
(1 - 2 minutes)
2. Review the Ground Rules.
(1 - 2 minutes)
3. Introduce the topic. (1 - 2 minutes)
4. Each member may speak to the topic.
(5 - 15 minutes)
5. Optional: Review what was said.
(3 - 5 minutes)
6. Summary discussion. (2 - 8 minutes)
7. Close the circle. (Less than one minute.)

Chart Four:

Ground Rules for the Circle Session

1. Bring yourself to the circle and nothing else.
2. Everyone gets a turn to share including the leader.
3. You can skip your turn if you wish.
4. Listen to the person who is speaking.
5. The time is shared equally.
6. Stay in your own space.
7. There are no interruptions, probing, put-downs, or gossip.

8. What is discussed in the circle stays in the circle.

Directions:

Part One

1. Provide the students with a brief descriptive overview of the program. In your own words explain: *The activity we are going to do today has several purposes. First, it will give us another chance to get to know each other better by using our speaking and listening skills. Second, it will introduce you to the program our class is starting. This program has many activities that will help us become even better communicators. It will teach us about anger management, understanding the influences in our lives — other people and media influences, how to prevent violence before it starts, and how to create a peaceful and harmonious classroom and school. The program has two main types of activities. The first type consists of all sorts of experiences like task groups, general discussions, dramatizations and role plays, even lessons that you will teach each other. The activity we're about to do is in this category. It's a dyad activity in which you will talk with three different partners and listen as they speak. The second main type of activity in the program is called a 'circle session,' a discussion in a small group. The process, or procedure, of all circle sessions is always the same, but each one has a different topic. After we finish the dyads I'll tell you why we are going to do circle sessions and how they work. Then we will have our first one.*

2. Help the students form groups of six members — breaking up troublesome pairs and making other necessary adjustments, or have them meet with classmates from a list you have prepared. It is important that the number in each group is an even number.

3. Ask the groups of students to move their chairs or desks into circles. Direct them to "pair up" with one of the people seated next to them by turning their chairs or desks so they are facing each other and to help make sure that everyone in their group has a partner. As soon as the dyads are formed, ask them to take five seconds to decide who will be A and who will be B. Ask for a show of hands for each category to be sure all of the students know their role and are committed to it.

4. There are three dyad "rounds." Point out the topics on Chart One and begin Round One by explaining: *Each of you will have one minute to speak as the other listens. The A's will speak first. B's will just listen with very little or no comment. If you are an A your topic is: 'A Favorite Musical Group or Song of Mine.' Speak for the whole minute if you can. Tell your partner who you really like to listen to and why or if it's a song tell about why you like it so much. I'll let you know when the minute is up and then it will be B's turn to speak to the next topic. Begin.*

5. Stop the speakers at the one minute point and direct the B's to speak to the second topic: "A Favorite Game or Sport of Mine." Elaborate: *This could be a sport you play yourself, or have played. You could be good at it or not. It could be a sport you like to watch instead of play. Tell why you like it as much as you do.*

6. Stop the speakers at the end of this minute. This is the end of the first round. Begin Round Two by directing the students to change partners by turning their chairs or desks to face the person who is on their other side in the circle and to decide again who will be A and who will be B with their new partners.

7. When the students are ready, lead the second round by having the A's take one minute to speak to the third topic: "A Favorite Book or Story of Mine." Elaborate: *Think back to something you have read that you really liked. Tell your partner about it and why you liked it.* At the end of one minute direct the B's to speak to the fourth topic: "A Favorite Movie or TV Show of Mine." Elaborate: *You probably have lots of these, but see if you can pick one and describe it briefly. Tell your partner what you like about it.*

8. Begin Round Three. First, direct the students to pair up with someone they haven't spoken with in a dyad yet and to sit facing that person. When they have determined who is A and who is B, direct the A's to speak to the fifth topic: "A Favorite Famous Person." Elaborate: *Take a minute to think about someone who everyone knows about, living or dead, who you really admire and respect. Tell your partner what the person did or what he or she stands for that impresses you.* At the end of one minute direct the B's to speak to the sixth topic: "A Favorite Non-Famous Person of Mine." Elaborate: *Tell your partner about someone you know, or know of, who has never made headlines but to you the person is very important. Explain why he or she matters to you.*

Here's a synopsis:

Round One:

- Establish first dyad partners — someone they are seated next to in their circles

- A speaks for one minute: "A Favorite Musical Group or Song of Mine," B listens.

- B speaks for one minute: "A Favorite Game or Sport of Mine," A listens.

Round Two:

- Change dyad partners — the person seated on their other side in their circles.

- A speaks for one minute: "A Favorite Book or Story of Mine," B listens.

- B speaks for one minute: "A Favorite Movie or TV Show of Mine," A listens.

Round Three:

- Change dyad partners — another member of their group

- A speaks for one minute: "A Favorite Famous Person of Mine," B listens.

- B speaks for one minute: "A Favorite Nonfamous Person of Mine," A listens

9. Reflect on the experience. Ask the students to remain where they are seated. Lead a short discussion by asking:

What was it like for you when you were the speaker in this activity?

What was it like as the listener?

Did you learn some new, interesting things about the people you met with?

How did you like changing partners and having a chance to communicate with three different people?

10. Express your appreciation to the students for their active participation and explain: *In a few minutes you will have a circle session with the people in your group. This activity may have helped you get ready for it by having you get used to topics and by speaking with three of the people in your group already. Sometimes*

things like this might seem difficult, but this is how we learn to be better communicators — by doing it. This class is all about learning to live and living to learn!

Part Two

11. Call the attention of the students to Charts Two, Three and Four. Read and review each one for the class elaborating on those points that are particularly important for your group.

12. Direct the groups to have their first circle session with the topic: "A Favorite Place of Mine." (See next page.) Have each group select a leader. Then "walk" them through the process, by circulating and announcing the steps to assist the leaders as the groups carry out their sessions simultaneously. They will need to select leaders who will need your assistance by "walking them through" the process step-by-step. As soon as this is done one or two more times, the students will know the process and will be able to conduct their groups independently.

Note: A preferred alternative if time permits would be to conduct a demonstration circle session first: Sit down with one of the groups and become its leader. Ask all of the other students to gather around to watch and listen as your group discusses "A Favorite Place of Mine." After the demonstration, direct the students to re-form their circles with their group members to hold simultaneous circle sessions with the topic: "A Time When I Was Pleasantly Surprised." As stated above in step 12, they will need to select leaders who will need your assistance by "walking them through" the process step-by-step.

A Favorite Place of Mine
A Circle Session

Objectives:

— to serve as an enjoyable introduction to the process

— to allow the students to continue to get to know and appreciate each other

After setting the tone and reviewing the ground rules, introduce the topic in your own words:

This is our first circle session and our topic is one I'm sure you'll like. It is: 'A Favorite Place of Mine.' Think about places you have been that you really like. The place that comes to your mind might be one you've only been to once or twice like a special spot in a park, or at a beach, or in a national forest. Or you might be thinking about a place you go to frequently maybe even every day. It could be a place in your home or yard or maybe at a friend's house. This could even be an imaginary place or a place you've only seen in photos or on TV

and at times you go there in your mind. Sometimes it helps to picture a place you like if you close your eyes. If you choose to speak in this circle session tell us about the place you are thinking about and how you feel when you are there. Let's take a few moments to think about the topic. When you are looking at me, I'll know you are ready to continue. Again, the topic is: 'A Favorite Place of Mine.'

Summary Discussion Questions:

— Did you notice any similar characteristics in the places we told each other about?

— When someone described a place, were you able to see it in your mind's eye?

— What are the benefits of having a circle session like this one?

A Time When I Was Pleasantly Surprised
A Circle Session

Objectives:

— to serve as another enjoyable introduction to the process

— to allow the students to continue to get to know and appreciate each other

After setting the tone and reviewing the ground rules, introduce the topic in your own words:

This is our second circle session and I'm sure you will enjoy this topic too. It is: 'A Time When I Was Pleasantly Surprised.' Can you remember a time like this when something unexpected happened and you liked it? Maybe it was just a thing like coming home to find that your favorite food was cooking on the stove. Or maybe it was something really special like having your family and your friends give you a surprise birthday party. Perhaps you got a higher grade on a test or in a class than you thought you would. Take a few moments to think about it. If you decide to take a turn, tell us what it was and how it made you feel. The topic is, 'A Time When I Was Pleasantly Surprised.'

Summary Discussion Questions:

— Did you notice any similarities in the pleasant surprises we told each other about and how they caused us to feel?

— Did anyone tell about something you could really relate to? If so, what was it?

— What does a circle session do for us?

DID I HEAR YOU RIGHT?
Brainstorming, Dyads and Discussion
A Fundamental Activity

The purposes of this activity are to sharpen the students' awareness of the value of speaking and listening effectively and to identify, and practice, specific speaking and listening skills as well as actions to avoid.

Description:

Students brainstorm and create a chart identifying specific skills used and actions avoided by effective speakers and listeners. The next part of the activity has two dyad rounds for using and practicing the skills they identified. The activity is concluded by adding more input to the chart and with a general class discussion about the importance of listening carefully.

Objectives:

Students will:

— identify skills used by effective speakers and listeners as well as actions they avoid.

— speak and listen to two different partners in dyad discussions.

— as listeners, repeat back to their partners what they heard to make sure they heard correctly.

— give and listen to feedback from their partners regarding possible listening inaccuracies.

— participate in a class discussion regarding the importance of using speaking and listening skills and what those skills are.

Time needed:

One class period.

(Continued, next page.)

Preparations needed:

Before class prepare the following chart on the chalkboard:

GOOD SPEAKERS	GOOD LISTENERS
Use these skills:	Use these skills:
Avoid these actions:	Avoid these actions:

Additionally, write these topics on the chalkboard for students to begin thinking about before the activity:

"One of the Best Things that's Happened to Me So Far this Week"

"Something I'm Looking Forward to (or Hope Will Happen)"

Directions:

1. Open this activity with brainstorming by asking the students: *Think about people you know who generally communicate with other people well. See if you can come up with what it is they do and don't do. Let's start with the skills they use as speakers and then we can focus on the actions they avoid when they are speaking. Let me go first.* Write a brief description of a skill you have noticed effective speakers use. Here's a suggestion: *I'm going to write: 'They tell you what's on*

their mind.' Most people are willing to actually speak. However, certain others won't communicate at all and that's one sure way to be a poor communicator. Who else has an idea?

2. Fill in all four segments of the chart with the students' input. It's okay if the spaces are not completely filled in because they will return to it later at the end of the activity to add more ideas. Point out to the students: *Taking time to figure out what good communicators do and don't do is worthwhile. It's also good for everyone to practice effective speaking and listening skills whenever possible. Being a good communicator is one of the most useful life skills you could possibly have. Perhaps you've noticed that the people who communicate well with others are likely to have the most success in their jobs and good relationships even if they aren't the smartest or best looking people. Likewise, some people who*

are very smart and good looking and maybe even rich but don't communicate with others well are likely to be less successful and usually not as happy in their lives. Today we're going to narrow our focus on both speaking and listening skills with a special emphasis on the art of listening.

3. Ask: *Why do you think some people think listening is even more important than speaking?* Listen to their responses and add a few of your own. Possibilities: In conversations people can create difficulties for themselves by speaking but not by listening. When you are speaking (on "transmit") you aren't receiving new information or learning anything. But you can find out vital information when you listen.

4. Review ways to listen effectively: *Just simply stop talking and hear what the other person is saying. Do not "transmit;" stay quiet. Just listen without thinking about what you want to say next. We do this in our circle sessions so the one who is speaking has a green light to speak with no distractions to stop him or her. In other situations like ordinary conversations it sometimes helps to ask questions if you don't understand something or if the person seems to need help to say what he or she is trying to say. But too many questions can overwhelm or annoy a speaker. When good listeners tune in to a speaker they 'mentally record' what the person is saying kind of like a tape recorder. Today we are going to practice these listening skills.*

5. Begin Round One by asking the students to "pair up" with another student in the class to form dyads. As soon as they are seated facing each other, ask them to take five seconds to decide who will be A and who will be B. Ask for a show of hands for each category to be

sure all of the students know their role and are committed to it.

6. Point to the first topic on the chalk-board, "One of the Best Things That's Happened to Me So Far This Week" and explain: *Here's how this activity will work: The A's are going to have two minutes to speak to this topic. Try your best to talk for the full two minutes and to speak as clearly and directly as you can to help your partner understand you. B's, you will listen quietly and record in your minds what you hear your partners say. Don't ask any questions unless you don't understand something or if you think A needs some help. At the end of the two minutes I'll let you know. Then B's, you will take one minute to tell your partner what you heard him or her say and to ask, 'Did I hear you right?' I'll let you know when that minute is up. Then A's, you will take one half minute to make any corrections to your partners to let them know what they may not have heard correctly. You may also compliment them on a job well done if they listened well. Any questions? Let's begin.*

7. Follow the process described in #6 above. When complete, direct the A's and B's to change roles and to go through the same process again with the same topic. Be sure to announce all times and changes.

8. Begin Round Two by directing the students to find new dyad partners and to repeat steps 6 and 7, above, with the topic: "Something I'm Looking Forward to (or Hope Will Happen)."

Here's a synopsis:

Round One:

- Establish first dyad partners.

- A speaks for two minutes: "One of the

Best Things that's Happened to Me So Far this Week," B listens.

- B speaks for one minute telling A what he/she heard A say.

- A speaks for one half minute to make corrections and to compliment B.

- B speaks for two minutes: same topic. A listens.

- A speaks for one minute telling B what he/she heard B say.

- B speaks for one half minute to make corrections and/or to compliment A.

Round Two:

- Establish second dyad partners.

- A speaks for two minutes: "Something I'm Looking Forward to (or Hope Will Happen)," B listens.

- B speaks for one minute telling A what he/she heard A say.

- A speaks for one half minute to make corrections and to compliment B.

- B speaks for two minutes: same topic. A listens.

- A speaks for one minute telling B what he/she heard B say.

- B speaks for one half minute to make corrections and/or to compliment A.

9. Close the activity with a discussion. Ask the class:

After doing this activity do some new ideas come to your mind for the chart we started filling in regarding the skills used and actions avoided by good speakers and listeners?

When you were the speaker what were you aware of as you spoke?

When you were the listener did you 'mentally record' what your partner said correctly or did he or she have to make a lot of corrections?

What worked best for you as the listener, just listening, or listening and asking a few questions?

Why is it so important for people to learn how to listen well?

When you are talking with someone how can you tell if he or she is really listening? Let's focus again on what good listeners do and avoid doing.

If the students have not mentioned non-verbal communication behaviors up to this point it is likely they will now especially when responding to the final question, above. Tell them that the next activity will focus on "body language" and how it affects communication.

Extension for all grade levels:

Challenge the students to:

(1) observe and evaluate the listening skills they see demonstrated by characters in TV shows and movies. Suggest they notice what good and poor listeners create in their relationships by their actions.

(2) use the skills they practiced in this activity over the next few days with their friends and members of their families.

Set aside some time at the beginning of a class session in three or four days to ask the students to share observations and anecdotes. Share an observation and an anecdote of your own with the class.

Someone Listened to Me When I Needed It

A Circle Session

Objective:

— to enable the students to recognize the fact that everyone needs, and deserves, to be listened to.

After setting the tone and reviewing the ground rules, introduce the topic in your own words:

Today our topic for our circle session is an important one. It has to do with the importance of being listened to. The topic is, 'Someone Listened to Me When I Needed It.' We all know how awful it can feel when someone we really want to communicate with us won't listen and how much we appreciate it when they will. Can you think of a situation that you would be comfortable telling us about — something that wouldn't embarrass you to share or us to hear — where someone or more than one person showed you the respect of listening to what you had to say? Perhaps their listening allowed you to do or have

something you really needed or wanted. Or maybe it was just important to you to be understood and for them to accept your feelings. If you decide to tell us about a time like this we would like to hear it. The topic is: 'Someone Listened to Me When I Needed It.'

Optional: After each circle member who wishes to speak has had a chance, conduct a review to reinforce listening skills (if time allows).

Summary Discussion Questions:

— *How did being listened to cause us to feel?*

— *What can occur when someone wants to be listened to and it doesn't happen?*

— *Does everyone need, and deserve, to be listened to?*

— *Did you notice or learn something in this session that you would like to mention?*

ACTIONS SPEAK LOUDER THAN WORDS!
Dyads, Impromptu Dramatizations and Discussion
A Fundamental Activity

The purpose of this activity is to increase the student's awareness of the powerful influence of nonverbal body language on the quality of interpersonal communication, and the specific effects of certain nonverbal actions.

Description:

Part One: Students form dyads and take turns speaking and listening to each other. As the speakers talk, the listeners withhold eye contact. The process is repeated exactly as before, but this time the listeners give eye contact as the speakers talk. Next, the teacher or counselor leads a class discussion about the importance of eye contact and asks what other nonverbal actions affect interpersonal communication. This leads to Part Two. As examples are generated, students are invited to demonstrate them in impromptu dramatizations.

Objectives:

Students will:

— speak and listen to partners in dyads giving and not giving each other eye contact.

— participate in a class discussion regarding the importance of eye contact and other nonverbal ways of communicating.

— enact and observe impromptu dramatizations of various nonverbal behaviors and their effect on the communication process.

Time needed:

25 to 35 minutes

Directions:

Part One

1. Begin by asking the students what they remember from the former activity about how to listen well as another person speaks. Explain: *We concluded that listening well is one of the most important skills you could possibly have. Besides just being quiet and not talking we learned about mentally recording what the other person is saying and how to ask questions if necessary but not to overdo the questions. Today we are going to have an experience with an entirely different aspect of communication.*

2. Direct the students to "pair up" with another student in the class to form dyads. As soon as they are seated facing each other, ask them to take five seconds to decide who will be A and who will be B. Ask for a show of hands for each category to be sure all of the students know their role and are committed to it.

3. Begin Round One: Explain: *The A's will speak for one minute to the B's. Your topic will be, 'What I Think of the Weather We've Been Having.' B's, as your partner speaks remain silent, stay in your seat, and look anywhere and everywhere except into his or her eyes. I'll let you know when the minute is up. Any questions? Begin.*

Note: As this happens expect the noise level in the room to increase dramatically because the speakers will raise their voices in an effort to get their partner's attention. Laughter is also guaranteed to occur.

4. At the end of the minute say, *Stop. Now B look at A and for one half minute listen as A tells you how that felt.*

5. Repeat steps 3 and 4, above, again. However, this time B looks at A as A speaks to the topic and as A tells B how that felt.

6. Round Two: Direct the students to reverse roles. The exact process in steps 3, 4 and 5 are repeated with B as the speaker and A as the listener. The topic is: "Something I Want to Accomplish This Week."

Here's a synopsis:

Round One: "What I Think of the Weather We've Been Having"

- One minute: A speaks to the topic. B gives no eye contact.

- One half minute: A tells B how that felt. B gives eye contact.

- One minute: A speaks to the topic again. B gives eye contact.

- One half minute: A tells B how that felt. B gives eye contact.

Round Two: "Something I Want to Accomplish This Week"

- One minute: B speaks to the topic. A gives no eye contact.

- One half minute: B tells A how that felt. A gives eye contact.

- One minute: B speaks to the topic again. A gives eye contact.

- One half minute: B tells A how that felt. A gives eye contact.

7. Thank the students for their active participation. Initiate discussion by asking them:

How did you feel when your partner wouldn't make eye contact with you?

What was it like when you did get eye contact from your partner?

Were you aware of how noisy the room became when eye contact was not being given? What caused that?

Eye contact is a nonverbal way of communicating. It has an enormously powerful effect on the quality of conversations. In our culture when it is given it helps communication; when it is not given it hurts it. Most people in our culture don't like it when someone withholds eye contact from them. When eye contact is withheld a lot it can be very damaging to relationships. There are other things people do with their eyes that help and hurt communication. Can you think of some of them?

(Examples: It helps when people smile with their eyes as well as their mouths at appropriate times in a conversation. It hurts if they look up at the ceiling when someone says something.)

Nonverbal communication is also sometimes called 'body language.' There are lots of ways we communicate messages and moods with our bodies. These actions often speak louder than words. Can you think of other forms of nonverbal communication or body language?

Part Two

8. With respect to the last point, above, invite students who respond with examples to perform impromptu dramatizations of the forms of nonverbal communication they mention. Make it fun. Assist them by playing the part of the "other person" in two-way communication situations. Examples: a wide variety of facial expressions, turning the body toward and away from a speaker, moving toward or away from a speaker, showing an "open" body posture, or demonstrating a "closed" body posture, and using assorted gestures.

Extension for all grade levels:

Discuss the fact that many nonverbal forms of body language convey different messages in different cultures. For example, the amount of eye contact that is generally accepted as appropriate throughout the United States and the western world is felt to be rude by many Japanese, Eskimos, Native Americans and Mexicans. Challenge the students to find out which cultures these are and to learn why this is true for them. The students may also be challenged to find out what various gestures convey in different parts of the world and what physical distances between people in a conversation are considered to be appropriate in different cultures. Underscore discussions with the principle that when interacting with individuals of different cultures it is wise to conform to their nonverbal communication expectations to the extent possible. Effective communicators are open-minded, flexible and adaptable.

A Time I 'Listened To' Body Language

A Circle Session

Objective:

— to provide an opportunity for the students to examine actual situations in which body language "spoke" to them and they "listened"

After setting the tone and reviewing the ground rules, introduce the topic in your own words:

We have been focusing on nonverbal communication, or 'body language' in our class lately and our topic is about this aspect of communication. It is: 'A Time I "Listened to" Body Language.' The fact is that whether we realize it or not we are constantly communicating nonverbally with one another and our bodies almost always tell the truth! Can you think of a time when you 'read' or 'listened to' someone's nonverbal message? Maybe they gestured to you and you understood the gesture. Perhaps they said one thing in words but their body said something else. An example of this could have been a real situation in your own life or maybe it was an actor or actress you were watching in a movie or TV show. If you decide to speak today, tell us about a situation you would feel comfortable describing. It may be best not to tell us who the person was in your story. Give it some thought. The topic is: 'A Time I "Listened To" Body Language.'

Optional: After each circle member who wishes to speak has had a chance, conduct a review to reinforce listening skills (if time allows).

Summary Discussion Questions:

— *If someone says one thing but their body language says another which message do you trust most?*

— *Is it possible to become more conscious of what your body is saying so you can be more successful and happy in your relationships with other people?*

— *Did you notice or learn something in this session that you would like to mention?*

THE COMMUNICATION STOPPERS!
Demonstration Role Plays and Discussion
A Fundamental Activity

The purpose of this activity is to pinpoint in the student's awareness certain common habits that are particularly destructive to the flow of communication. With this awareness students may be less prone to commit these actions during circle sessions and in general interpersonal situations.

Description:

The teacher/counselor presents a list of behaviors that typically stop or retard communication and demonstrates them by briefly role-playing each one with a student. A class discussion follows each demonstration.

Objectives:

Students will:

— observe and participate in role play demonstrations of behaviors that generally block communication and discuss the outcomes of each one.

— discuss how the use of communication stoppers in conversations generally affect speakers behaviorally and emotionally.

Time needed:

30 to 40 minutes.

Preparations Needed:

Write the following list on the chalkboard or chart paper:

- Interrupting
- Dominating
- Judging
- Probing
- Giving Unasked-for Advice
- Misinterpreting
- Accusing/Contradicting/Criticizing
- Putting Down/Name-calling/
  Ridiculing

Directions:

1. Begin by asking the students to think of a heading or title for the above list. Write their suggestions on the board and discuss each one briefly. Add the suggested title: "The Communication Stoppers."

2. Suggest: *Let's take a good look at these and see how they affect someone who is trying to communicate. Probably all of us have used these from time to time. You aren't a bad person if you have ever used them. In fact, in some situations some of them might be appropriate but they almost always stop communication. They ruin circle sessions*

and they ruin many conversations. I'm going to need eight volunteers to help me demonstrate these so we can see their effect on someone who is trying to speak to someone else. I'll be that 'someone else.' Each volunteer will need to have something in mind to tell me about. It could be about almost anything — a vacation your family took, the funniest thing your pet does, what you think of something that's going on in the news, etc. Each volunteer should talk to me as long as possible about your subject or until I call time. I will demonstrate one of the 'communication stoppers' and then the class will guess which one it was. Who will volunteer?

3. List the names of eight volunteers on the board. (If eight don't volunteer allow those who do to have more than one turn.) Then invite them to the front of the class one-by-one. After each demonstration ask:

   Which 'stopper' do you think I was attempting to demonstrate?

   (To the volunteer): *If this had been a real situation how would my responses have made you feel?*

   Has this ever happened to you? What did you say or do?

4. Begin the demonstrations. Use appropriate gestures, volume, and tone, and make your responses as convincing as possible. Continue to use examples of the particular communication stopper you are demonstrating until the student gives up or the point has been sufficiently made.

   Here are suggestions for how to demonstrate each communication stopper and specific questions to ask the class regarding each one: (Suggestions: demonstrate the communication stoppers in a different order than the order shown here. Select students with strong personalities who volunteer to demonstrate the communication stoppers, especially for the last two, below.)

Interrupting

Demonstration: Butt in time and again as the student talks with statements about yourself and things that have happened to you. For example, if the student says, *Last summer my family took a vacation. We went to...* interrupt with a statement (not a question) such as, *Hey, that reminds me I haven't told you about my last vacation yet. I went to.... etc., etc.* Interrupt at least three times in this manner.

Discussion: Talk about how frustrating it is to be interrupted and how futile it is to continue a conversation with a chronic interrupter. Interrupting is probably the most common way to stop communication and if it keeps happening it will stop it for sure sooner or later. Interrupters usually don't realize what they are doing and probably wonder from time to time why their conversations go flat.

Dominating

Demonstration: Take over the conversation beginning with one interruption and don't stop talking and don't let the student volunteer get in another word. If he or she says, *Last summer my family took a vacation. We went to...* Jump in and say, *Oh, is that so? Well my family took one too. We went to... blah... blah... blah...*

Discussion: Mention how discouraging it is to try to have a conversation with a dominator who seems to need so much attention that he or she doesn't have a sense of how to engage in natural "give and take" in a conversation. Rather, the dominator just takes over. The more people avoid them the more dominators want to make contact with other people and dominate in those conversation. This continues until perhaps something might happen to let them know what they are in the habit of doing.

Judging

Demonstration: Be judgmental. Evaluate what the student volunteer says and the student him/herself. For example, if the student says, *Last summer my family took a vacation. We went to a resort*, say, *That's not a worthwhile place to go to for a vacation. There's nothing educational about it.* If the student continues, saying, *I didn't want to go at first but then I agreed to go along.* Say, *How wonderful! What a good person you are to go with your family even though you didn't really want to at first.*

Discussion: Talk with the students about how no one likes to be around judgmental people. Even when judgments are positive the one judging is acting superior. Judging often leads to arguments and usually ends conversations. Judgmental people are often lonely people.

Probing

Demonstration: Interrogate the student volunteer with one question after another. If the student says, *Last summer my family took a vacation. We went to...* jump in and ask, *Say, how many vacations does your family take in a year?* When he or she starts to answer, ask more questions such as, *Why did you choose to go there? Don't you think your family overdoes the vacations?* etc.

Discussion: Discuss with the students the difference between probing and the natural and comfortable way questions are asked in a normal conversation. Even under the best of circumstances questions can take speakers away from where they originally intended to go with their remarks and when questions are overdone they tend to put speakers on the defensive. This usually makes them want to leave the conversation. (These are the reasons questions are not asked during circle sessions and are held until they have been closed.)

Giving Unasked-for Advice

Demonstration: Tell the student volunteer all sorts of things he or she should or should not do despite the fact that your advice was not solicited. If the student says, *Last summer my family took a vacation. We went to my uncle's farm*, tell the student, *Oh, you shouldn't have gone there. Take my advice: on your next vacation you should go to Yellowstone or some place like that. If I were you I'd choose a place where there's more to see and do than...*

Discussion: Talk with the students about how, like judging, giving unasked-for advice places the adviser in a superior position. Who wants to continue to communicate with someone who acts this way? Sadly, people who do this probably just want to feel important and may even mean to be helpful. They just don't seem to realize the effects they are having.

Misinterpreting

Demonstration: Twist everything around that the student volunteer says: For example, if he or she says, *Last summer my family took a vacation. We went to the mountains...*, say, *So, you had to get away from your normal life.* If he or she objects and says, *No, that's not it. We just wanted some time with each other in a beautiful place,* respond with, *Oh, are you having serious family troubles and you found it necessary to ignore your problems for awhile?*

Discussion: By analyzing and trying to interpret what someone is saying, this person shows that he or she is unwilling to accept what the other person says at face value. No one likes being in conversations with people who do this and most people will get away from them as soon as they can.

Accusing/Contradicting/Criticizing

Demonstration: Contradict what the student volunteer says and accuse him or her of being wrong. For example, if he or she says, *Last summer my family took a vacation. We went river rafting,* say *You're lying. You did not go river rafting. I know because I talked with your sister and she said you went to Mexico. You really ought to clean up your act and tell the truth to people.*

Discussion: This is one of the most destructive of all of the communication stoppers. Talk with the students about how contradictions, accusations and criticism rarely help a situation. Even if you have "the goods" on someone this approach usually makes the other person become hostile. No one likes to be called wrong or bad even when they are guilty. There are other ways to respond to people than to accuse, contradict or criticize them unless you want to make them mad and stop communication. Using this communication stopper almost always results in a lose-lose outcome.

Putting Down/Name-calling/Ridiculing

Demonstration: Make sarcastic, negative remarks in response to everything the student says. For example, if he or she says, *Last summer my family took a vacation. We went to ...* say, *Who cares? You're a bum, always going off on your idiotic vacations. Only wierdos are always taking off like that. Get a life.*

Discussion: This is the most destructive of all the communication stoppers. Discuss with the students how it insults and diminishes the speaker and can create deep feelings of resentment within him or her. Even when a put down is done as a joke it may not be so funny to the one who is the butt of the joke.

A Time I Held My Tongue

A Circle Session

Objective:

— to allow students to share incidents in which they used restraint to their advantage in sensitive communication situations

After setting the tone and reviewing the ground rules, introduce the topic in your own words:

Recently we have been learning about negative communication habits that stop communication. Our topic today is not about how you may have done one of these things, but rather how you didn't. The topic is, 'A Time I Held My Tongue.' See if you can remember a time when you really felt like saying something negative to someone or you caught yourself about to interrupt, or give some advice to someone who didn't ask for it. Perhaps you were about to use another one of those other communication stoppers that cause people who wish to communicate to shut down or leave. If

you decide to take a turn to speak, tell us about the situation and what you almost did, just don't tell us who the other person was. Do tell us about the result of your ability to control yourself, however, and how you feel about it now. The topic is: 'A Time I Held My Tongue.'

After each circle member who wishes to speak has had a chance, conduct a review to reinforce listening skills (if time allows).

Summary Discussion Questions:

— *What was similar about most or all of the situations we discussed?*

— *How did most or all of us feel about having held our tongues? What might have happened otherwise to the other people and to us?*

— *Did you notice or learn something in this session that you would like to mention?*

LISTEN WITH THE THIRD EAR!
Presentation, Handout Assignment and Discussion
A Fundamental Activity

The purposes of this activity are to enlighten students about incongruities that frequently exist in individuals' statements between what they vocalize and what they actually mean, and to enable them to begin learning how to respond to real meanings in such a way that potential difficulties might be avoided.

Description:

Part One: The students are presented with two brief scenarios to which they are asked to state their first reactions and to consider the behaviors of one of the characters in the scenarios. They then generate a response the other character might make to pave the way for understanding. Finally, the students are presented with strategies for "listening with the third ear."

Part Two: The students complete the handout, "What are They Really Saying?" and conclude with a group discussion.

Objectives:

Students will:

— listen to, read about, and discuss common interpersonal situations in which a person says one thing but actually means something else, and attempt to determine the real feelings, needs and motives behind the statement.

— listen to and discuss strategies for "listening with the third ear" and how to respond to someone who is saying one

thing but means something else in a manner that will calm a potentially difficult situation.

— discuss the usefulness of "listening with the third ear" and responding to real meanings in calming ways in everyday situations.

Time needed:

30 to 40 minutes.

Materials needed:

One copy of the handout, "What are They Really Saying?" for each student

Directions:

Part One

1. Introduce the activity by reviewing with the class some of the key points they have learned about effective communication. Point out: *When you combine all of the listening, verbal and nonverbal skills we have learned so far, you are becoming a capable 'active communicator.' Today we are going to go a little deeper into the art of active communication by learning to 'listen with the third ear.'* Briefly discuss what this expression might mean by associating it with the expressions: "reading between the lines" and "looking beyond the surface."

2. After developing an understanding of the meaning of "listening with the third ear," read and discuss the following scenarios with the students:

• Catherine is a junior in high school and enjoys small children. Baby-sitting is one of her favorite ways to earn money. One evening she went to the home of a couple with a four-year-old boy, William. She had never baby-sat for this family before. As soon as Catherine was brought into the house by William's mother, William hid behind his mother's legs and wouldn't respond when Catherine said, "Hi, William. Are you going to be my friend tonight?" William's Mom urged him to speak but he refused. Finally, after his parents had gone William gave Catherine a very intense look and asked, "Do you hit little kids?"

Ask the following questions:

—*If you had been Catherine how would William's remark have affected you and what would you have felt like saying to him?*

—*What was bothering William and what did he really want to know?*

Listen to the students' responses and if they did not come up with it make sure you offer, *William really wanted to know, 'Will I be safe with you?' to which Catherine might have responded: 'I'm a nice baby-sitter, William, and I can see that you are a nice boy. I won't hurt you.'*

• Jose and Richard are high school seniors who frequently hang out together. Jose is the oldest and just got his license to drive but Richard still has his learner's permit. One afternoon Richard borrowed his Dad's truck and drove Jose out to the country where no one lived.

When he saw a dirt road going off from the highway, he took it saying, "I always wanted to know what was down this road. Let's take a look." Jose responded with a grin. Both of them were having a great time. After going about three miles, they came to a huge mud hole in the road and instead of stopping or trying to go around it Richard plowed in. Well, you know what happened. The truck got stuck in the mud. No matter what they tried, Jose and Richard just couldn't get the truck out. There was nothing else to do but hike the three miles back to the highway and try to get a ride to a phone so they could call for help. As they walked along, Jose kept saying, "What did I tell you? I knew something like this would happen. Didn't I tell you not to take this road?"

Ask the following questions:

—*If you had been Richard, how would Jose's remarks affect you and what would you have felt like saying to him?*

—*What was bothering Jose and what did he really mean?*

Listen to student's responses and if they didn't come up with it, make sure you offer, *Jose is older and had his license. He probably felt responsible and guilty. He was trying to get Richard to say, Nobody's blaming you for this, Jose.*

3. At the conclusion of the scenario discussions, present the following strategies for "listening with the third ear" to the students:

• Admit to yourself how you feel about what the person has said, but stop yourself from responding with the first thing that pops into your head.

• Ask yourself, "If I were him or her and I

had just said that why would I have said it?" Then give yourself an honest answer. Realize that the person is experiencing an uncomfortable emotion like embarrassment, insignificance, anger, fear, jealousy, insecurity or guilt.

- Calmly ask the person a question to help you understand what he or she is concerned about if you aren't sure, like: "Please tell me what's bothering you?"

- Figure out what you could say that might help the person feel better and say it in a kind way. Be prepared to say it again if necessary.

Part Two

4. Distribute the handout, "What are They Really Saying?" to the students (See next paget). Review it with them to make sure they understand the assignment. Explain that they may work on it alone or with a partner.

5. After the students have completed their handouts, review each one and their responses as a class.

Here are some responses to each of the scenarios:

Theresa and Suzy: You would probably feel exasperated at Theresa if you were Suzy and feel like telling her to ask her questions to the teacher herself. Theresa probably does this because she is afraid of making a fool of herself and being criticized. Suzy might say to her: "That's a good question, Theresa. Why don't you ask it? Everyone will probably appreciate it if you do."

Robert and Gustavo: You would probably be shocked and put off by Robert's reactions if you were Gustavo and feel like telling him he's off base. Robert probably reacted this way because his feelings are

still hurt by Gina breaking up with him and he may still want her back. Gustavo might tell him: "Hey, you're my friend, I'd never go out with her if you didn't want me to. I'll tell her right away."

Tina and Carlos: You would probably feel angry at Tina if you were Carlos and feel like yelling, "This time you're wrong, smarty!" Tina probably argues like this so often because she wants people to acknowledge how intelligent and knowledgeable she is. Carlos might tell her what she needs to hear and stop her in her tracks if he said: "It doesn't matter what kind of truck it is, Tina. You're smart and you know a lot. I'm proud to be your brother."

Karen and Fred: You would probably feel disgusted by Fred's complaints and excuses if you were Karen and feel like saying, "Stop moaning and groaning. Why don't you just admit you can't row without losing the oars?" Fred wants to be noticed and appreciated. He hates looking bad. Karen might cause him to feel better and possibly get him to stop making excuses by telling him, "It's okay. We're just out here to enjoy ourselves. So what if the oars keep getting away?"

6. Culminate the activity with a discussion by asking the students:

—*It can be hard to 'listen with the third ear' at times. What is the hardest thing about it for you?*

—*How can you overcome the difficulties of doing this?*

—*What is the value of being able to 'listen with the third ear?'*

—*Could people be more capable of saying what they really mean if they have learned to 'listen to others with the third ear?' How could it help them?*

WHAT ARE THEY REALLY SAYING?

Read each of the following scenarios. Then write a response to the questions at the end of each one:

Theresa and Suzy

Theresa and Suzy are friends and sit next to each other in class. Almost every day after their teacher gives them an assignment, Theresa tells Suzy to ask the teacher questions, such as, "Ask him when we have to turn it in?" or "Find out how many pages it has to be?"

If you were Suzy how would Theresa's actions affect you?

_____

What would you feel like telling her?

_____

_____

Why is Theresa doing this?

_____

_____

If you wanted to make her feel better and possibly get her to stop doing this what could you say to Theresa in a calm way?

_____

_____

■■■■■■■■■■■■■■■■■■■■■■■■■■■■■■■■■■■■■■

Robert and Gustavo

Robert and Gustavo are juniors in high school and are best friends. They recently had their girlfriends break up with them. One day, Robert's former girlfriend, Gina, approached Gustavo and asked him to a dance which was a girls' choice school activity. Gustavo was very surprised and hardly knew what to say. He told Gina he'd let her know. Later he saw Robert and told him about it. Robert turned red and started to shake. He bellowed at Gustavo, "You didn't tell her no? How could you do that to me? What kind of a friend are you?"

If you were Gustavo how would Robert's response affect you?

_____

What would you feel like saying to him?

_____

_____

Why did Robert act this way?

_____

_____

If you wanted to make Robert feel better, what could you calmly say to him?

_____

_____

■■■■■■■■■■■■■■■■■■■■■■■■■■■■■■■■■■■■■

Tina and Carlos

Tina and Carlos are brother and sister. Tina is fifteen and Carlos is thirteen. Like most sisters and brothers they love each other but arguments frequently occur between them and these arguments are usually over insignificant things. Just this morning they had been arguing for nearly an hour with Tina insisting she was right over and over again. Finally, to change the subject, Carlos noticed their neighbor pull out of his driveway in his new Chevy truck and mentioned that he really liked it. Tina said, "You never pay attention. It's not a Chevy; it's a Ford."

If you were Carlos how would Tina's incorrect statement affect you?

_____

_____

What would you feel like saying to her?

_____

_____

Why does Tina act this way so often?

_____

_____

If you wanted to make Tina feel better and end the argument what could you say to her in a calm way?

_____

_____

Karen and Fred

Karen and Fred are first cousins and their families vacation together at a cabin in the mountains every summer for a week. They are both fourteen years old and they like each other but Karen often wonders why Fred dresses in such outlandish clothes and dyes his hair bright orange. Not only that, Fred is always explaining himself and making excuses. He can't seem to admit that he ever makes mistakes just like everyone else. Just yesterday the two cousins decided to take a boat ride in a rental rowboat and Fred kept losing one or both oars when it was his turn to row. Whenever this happened Fred would complain: "These oarlocks are crummy. They don't hold the oars well. It's not my fault. I can't help it. Why can't they make these things work right?"

If you were Karen how would Fred's complaints and excuses affect you?

_____

What would you feel like saying to him?

_____

_____

Why does Fred probably act this way so often?

_____

_____

If you wanted to make Fred feel better and possibly get him to stop making excuses what could you say in a calm way?

_____

_____

A Time I Listened to Someone's Feelings

A Circle Session

Objective:

— to allow students to share incidents in which they focused on more than words in conversations with other people and heard their feelings and responded to those feelings.

After setting the tone and reviewing the ground rules, introduce the topic in your own words:

Our topic for today is 'A Time I Listened to Someone's Feelings.' We've been concerned recently with learning to listen to more than the words people speak by 'listening with the third ear' to identify their feelings and what their needs are. Can you think of a situation that occurred recently or some time back where you did this and responded to the feelings you could tell the person was having? Perhaps a friend needed your attention or was feeling angry about something and you caused him or her to feel better by what you said in response to his or her feelings. Or maybe it was someone in your family and they were feeling

embarrassed or insecure and you responded to the feelings instead of the words. Tell us about what happened and how you feel about it now if you decide to take a turn, but please don't tell us who the person was. The topic is: 'A Time I Listened to Someone's Feelings.'"

After each circle member who wishes to speak has had a chance, conduct a review to reinforce listening skills (if time allows).

Summary Discussion Questions:

— What is helpful to remember when these kinds of situations come up?

— How did most or all of us feel now about these times when we listened to other peoples' feelings and responded to their feelings?

— Did you notice or learn something in this session that you would like to mention?

How Positive Self Talk Helped Me

A Circle Session

Objectives:

— to assist the students to understand the powerful role of self talk in their lives

— to understand how self talk can help or hurt them.

After setting the tone and reviewing the ground rules, introduce the topic in your own words:

Today we are going to talk about a very serious and important matter: self-talk. The topic is, 'How Positive Self Talk Helped Me.' You may not realize it, but you talk to yourself all of the time even if you never say a word out loud. All of us do. We are either saying things to ourselves that challenge us, or encourage us, or make us justifiably proud of ourselves, or we are telling ourselves to forget about trying, to give up, or call ourselves names and put ourselves down. Self talk is very powerful. Many professionals like athletes, business people, and actors train themselves to use positive self talk. Can you think of a time when you talked to yourself and you knew you were doing it and you said things that turned

out to be helpful? Give it some thought and see if you can remember a time you did that. If you'd like to tell us about it we would be pleased to hear what you said to yourself and what the results were. The topic is, 'How Positive Self Talk Helped Me.'

After each circle member who wishes to speak has had a chance, conduct a review to reinforce listening skills (if time allows).

Summary Discussion Questions:

— What were some of the positive statements you heard in this session that you could use for yourself?

— What should you do if you catch yourself in negative self talk?

— Besides turning negative self talk around and making it positive what else can you do to train yourself to use positive self talk?

ANGER CAN BE MANAGED!

OVERVIEW . . .

The first step in managing anger is to develop the language and vocabulary that enables full discussion of the nature of anger: its forms, dangers, and possibilities for usefulness. As this unit unfolds, this language is utilized to foster the awareness and understanding necessary to achieve the second step in anger management: developing the ability to decide how to channel behavior when angry feelings occur instead of blindly and impulsively reacting with behavior that may be destructive. The ultimate goal is to empower students to develop their own internal guidelines for how to recognize anger and handle it within themselves.

Through a variety of active processes, this instructional unit has been designed to provide learning experiences that teach the following information or "understandings" about anger:

- Anger is a normal internal feeling usually experienced as a reaction to an external situation or event.

- Everyone has a right to feel anger, including times when someone's anger is in response to something you have done.

- The feeling of anger may spur behavior that is unproductive and destructive or productive and constructive. The feeling and the behavior are not the same thing.

- Many types and degrees of anger may be felt in relation to various situations and events.

- People experience anger, and all emotions, uniquely; different people feel differently about the same situation or event. Understanding this is the basis for acceptance and respect for oneself and others.

- Anger generally comes from fear or anxiety and often its expression causes more fear.

- People tend to imitate others they spend time with. Behavioral responses to angry feelings are often unexamined imitations.

- The ability to recognize one's anger and to think about it allows people to "talk with themselves" and make rational decisions regarding how to channel and use their anger.

- Denying anger within oneself is not healthy because it only remains hidden until something happens to cause the anger to express itself in behavior. Often this expression is destructive.

- Holding in the expression of anger can be unhealthy because the ultimate expression may be overblown or unfairly displaced on someone, or something, other than the actual cause of the anger.

- It is usually constructive whenever possible to respectfully and rationally discuss angry feelings and why one is having them with the person(s) responsible for those feelings.

- Physical activity generally dissipates strong anger allowing for greater ability to understand and use it.

- Anger can be used as a force to generate courage and motivation to achieve constructive goals.

An important resource for the development of this unit and an excellent source of additional information: *The Anger Workbook* by Lorrainne Bilodeau, M.S., Center City, Minnesota: Hazelden Educational Materials, 1992. Phone: (800) 328-9000.

Booklets for Students: *The Close Call* by Gerry Dunne, Ph.D. Torrance, CA: Jalmar press, 2001. Phone (800) 662-9662.

WHAT IS ANGER? — AN INTRODUCTION
Brainstorming, Categorizing and Defining
An Introductory Activity

Note to teachers and counselors:

*Humor grows on the fresh graves of anxiety.** Although this unit on managing anger is a very serious one, laughter will undoubtedly surface from time to time. This is a healthy release and does not mean that students are reacting frivolously to the subject matter. Laughter will, in fact, facilitate these learning experiences. When appropriate, laugh with your students when those funny moments inevitably occur, then refocus and guide them to form the critical understandings this unit provides.

The purpose of this activity is to enable students to acknowledge and begin to explore the often perplexing and mysterious emotion of anger with the guidance and assurance of their teacher or counselor. It is an important forerunner activity to those which follow because it allows students to collectively set forth their ideas, feelings, impressions and opinions about anger in a matter-of-fact manner and then to begin to make sense of them.

Description:

After a brief introduction about anger, the students are invited to state every word or phrase they can think of that relates to anger. Next the class examines these words and phrases and categorizes them into five categories. Last, they develop a definition of anger.

Objectives:

Students will:

— experience personal reactions relating to anger and state these aloud in a brainstorming activity.

— examine a mixed collection of words and phrases related to anger that have been generated by the class and place them into the categories of feelings, behaviors, thoughts, situations and metaphors.

— collaborate with class members and their teacher/counselor to develop a definition of anger.

Time needed:

30 to 50 minutes.

Materials needed:

Chart paper and magic marker (or chalk and chalkboard) for listing words and phrases generated by the class and one large strip of paper and magic marker for the definition of anger to be posted on a bulletin board.

Directions:

1. Introduce this activity with a brief story or example of a noteworthy, but not tragic, incident involving angry behavior of an unidentifiable person. Then

ask the class what the person was feeling. In your own words, point out: *Anger is a feeling we all get from time to time. Sometimes things people do when they are angry are understandable and healthy, but sometimes anger leads to very serious and terrible consequences. Many people have been hurt including innocent victims and the angry person him or herself. Anger is one of the most important things we can learn about at school so that we can use what we learn in our personal lives. Today we are going to start that process.*

2. Ask the students to think about anger. Explain: *Raise your hand as soon as you think of something about anger and I will write it down. It could be one word or a phrase and it could be about how you feel when you are angry or how you feel when someone else is angry. Please don't mention any names. Your word or phrase could be about how people act when they are angry, or what you think about those actions. Perhaps your word or phrase will be about things, or situations, that make you or others angry. And maybe you are thinking about something that reminds you of anger — like a tidal wave. Each of you can state as many words and phrases that come to your mind as you wish. Just be sure they are "classroom appropriate."*

3. Record the words and phrases with little comment except to acknowledge each student for each contribution.

4. When the students are through responding, express your appreciation and help them categorize the words and phrases into the five categories of feelings, behaviors, thoughts, situations and metaphors. Tell them: *Thanks for all the good input! Now, let's make some sense out of this. Can you see some categories here? For example, I see some words and phrases that are the names, or labels, for angry feelings and some others that are thoughts — opinions and ideas — about anger. Do you see any other categories?* Write the names of these five categories on a separate chart or space on the board.

5. Categorize each word and phrase by guiding the class through a coding process. Taking each one in turn help them to identify it. Place an F beside each type of angry feeling, a B beside each behavior (or action), a T beside each thought (idea or opinion), an S beside each situation (or event), and an M beside each metaphor (or simile).

6. Last, guide and assist the students to develop a definition of anger. Acknowledge and challenge them: *Great job of categorizing! Now let's take it one step further. Let's put our heads together and use what we've learned so far to state exactly what anger is.* **The definition your class develops should clarify that anger is an internal feeling usually experienced as a reaction to an external situation or event.** Added ideas might include that sometimes people do things because they are feeling angry and these acts may be hurtful and unhealthy, or not, but the feeling and the behavior are separate entities. People have many thoughts about anger and sometimes thoughts produce anger, but the thought and the feeling are not the same thing. Also, many things (metaphors) remind us of the feeling of anger and anger-engendered behavior.

7. Post the final written definition in a visible spot where it can be easily seen. The next two activities will provide additional items which may be posted under the definition.

Extension for Elementary, Middle and High School Art:

Ask the students to express visual impressions of anger artistically without placing human forms in their pictures. These may be the metaphors generated in the brainstorming activity: tidal waves, volcanoes, hailstorms, or they might be abstract renderings of color, shape and form.

Extension for Middle and High School Language Arts:

Encourage the use of metaphors and similes in relation to the feelings and behaviors of anger with creative writing assignments. Allow the students to work in pairs to create vivid paragraphs or short stories so that they may capitalize on each other's creative ideas.

---

* Martin Grotjahn, M.D., *Beyond Laughter: Humor and the Subconscious*. New York: McGraw-Hill Book Company, 1970.

HOW ANGRY WOULD YOU BE . . . ?
Introspection, Responding, Categorizing and Discussion
A Fundamental Activity

The purpose of this activity is to help students understand that while it is normal for everyone to experience anger, it is also normal for each individual to experience anger (and all emotions) uniquely. This understanding is the basis for acceptance and respect for oneself and others. The second purpose of this activity is to provide students with essential language that can empower them, through awareness, to acknowledge what they are feeling in future instances. This awareness is necessary if one is to decide how to channel behavior when angry feelings occur instead of blindly and impulsively reacting with behavior that may be destructive.

Description:

After briefly reviewing the prior activity, students are reminded of some of the situations they talked about and asked how they would feel if they had encountered them personally, and then their responses are charted as feeling labels. Next, students categorize the labels of anger into degrees from mild to intense. Last, the class engages in a culminating discussion regarding what they are learning about anger.

Objectives:

Students will:

— reflect on anger-provoking situations and individually decide within themselves how they would feel if they encountered each one.

— express on a voluntary basis, and listen to, names or labels for angry feelings in response to varying situations and events.

— assist their classmates and teacher/ counselor to categorize an assortment of labels of anger into degrees of intensity.

— discuss the meaning of the activity and its implications for life situations.

Time needed:

20 to 40 minutes

Materials needed:

Chart paper and magic marker (or chalk and chalkboard) for listing feeling labels.

Directions:

1. Briefly review what the students did in the first activity in this unit. Remind them that they heard about some situations that produced anger from each other and from you. Explain: *We're going to 'revisit' some of these situations and here's the procedure: first we'll hear the story again, then each of us will decide on a feeling word that describes how we would feel inside if this happened to us. Then, on my signal, you may volunteer your word if you wish and I'll write it down. There will be complete respect for each other and the words we state while we develop a list of words or labels that describe types of anger. Are you ready?*

2. Begin by summarizing one of the stories heard briefly. Remind the students: *Without saying anything out loud at first, silently decide how you would feel. Would it have made you angry, and if so, how angry would you be if this happened to you?*

3. Wait about five seconds and invite responses by asking the students to raise their hands if they wish to volunteer their words. Record their terms without evaluation. At times volunteer your own terms. In case off-color language is used, record it by putting the first letter(s) of the word(s) on the board. Smile and move on.

4. Continue this process, summarizing situations yourself and allowing students to do so as well. As necessary, briefly relate new situations that were not heard in the prior activity.

5. When numerous terms have been offered and charted (vocabulary in this area is very plentiful), change the task to categorizing degrees of intensity of anger for the various terms generated by the students. For example, three categories and code letters may be used: M for mild (feeling states like "irritated" or "miffed"), S for strong (feeling states like "annoyed" or "exasperated"), and I for intense (feeling states like "furious" or "outraged").

6. Conclude by acknowledging the students for their concentration and assistance. Culminate by asking them the following questions for open discussion:

— *What did you notice about our individual responses to each of the situations? Did we all come up with the same word? What does this tell us about people in general?*

— *Why is it important for us to understand that anger is normal and everyone feels it from time to time, but that different people feel anger in different ways even when facing the same situation?*

— *When we are angry and we know lots of words to describe what we are feeling we can talk to ourselves about it. Why is this helpful?*

Guide this discussion to bring out the points offered at the outset in "The purpose of this activity..."

Extension:

Challenge the students to work in task groups to form a hierarchy of all of the anger terms they generated from mild to intense. These will probably be similar but it is unlikely that any two groups will produce the exact same lists. After the lists have been completed and posted point this out to the class.

A Time I Couldn't Help But Get Mad
A Circle Session

Objective:

— to allow students to acknowledge that anger is a normal human emotion which everyone has the right to feel from time to time.

After setting the tone and reviewing the ground rules, introduce the topic in your own words:

In class we have been focusing on anger recently and the subject of anger is what this circle session is about. The topic is: 'A Time I Couldn't Help But Get Mad.' This could be an incident that happened recently or when you were younger. Does something come to your mind right away or do you need to think about this awhile? If you are thinking of an incident that you feel okay telling us about, that's fine. But, if the situation you are thinking about might embarrass you or another person to tell, or you think it might embarrass

us to hear, it would be best to tell about something else. If you decide to take a turn tell us what happened that upset you and how you felt at the time. You might even tell us how you feel about it now. If you take a turn, tell us all about it, but please don't tell us the names of the people involved or your relationship to them. The topic is: 'A Time I Couldn't Help But Get Mad.'

After each circle member who wishes to speak has had a chance, conduct a review to reinforce listening skills (if time allows).

Summary Discussion Questions:

— Did you notice any similarities in the situations that caused us anger?

— Do any of us have different feelings now about the incidents?

— Is it okay to feel anger?

Someone Was Being Treated Unfairly and It Made Me Mad

A Circle Session

Objectives:

— to allow students to acknowledge again that anger is a normal human emotion and that unfairness is a typical provocation

— to discriminate between the feeling and resulting behavior which may be productive and constructive or unproductive and destructive.

After setting the tone and reviewing the ground rules, introduce the topic in your own words:

Anger has been a subject we've been concerned about lately in our class. This circle session also focuses on anger just like the activities we have been doing. The topic is: 'Someone Was Being Treated Unfairly and It Made Me Mad.' Does this topic make you think of a situation in which someone was not being treated fairly and it upset you? In fact, the person may have been you or it could have been someone else. This could have happened anywhere and it could have occurred at any time, maybe even years ago. If you decide to describe a situation like this tell us what the situation was and how you felt. Tell how other people seemed to feel about it too. We would like to hear about it, but please don't tell us who was involved beside yourself. The topic is: 'Someone Was Being Treated Unfairly and It Made Me Mad.'

After each circle member who wishes to speak has had a chance, conduct a review to reinforce listening skills (if time allows).

Summary Discussion Questions:

— Is it good that unfairness is so likely to cause anger?

— When legitimate angry feelings occur, like when unfairness happens, does it matter how people show their anger?

CONCLUSIONS ABOUT ANGER
Individual Writing, Task Groups and Class Discussion
A Fundamental Activity

The purpose of this activity is to assist students to reach reasonable conclusions about the fact that everyone rightfully has angry feelings, and that there are healthy/productive (emotionally mature) and unhealthy/unproductive (emotionally immature) responses to anger in others and in oneself.

Description:

After briefly reviewing the prior activities in this unit, the students are asked to write brief notes to themselves to a series of five questions about anger. Next, students meet in small task groups to collaborate in forming one-sentence responses. Each task group presents its "conclusion" and briefly describes how it was arrived at. The sessions end with the teacher/counselor asking additional thought-provoking questions and providing additional information.

Objectives:

Students will:

— individually contemplate and write notes to themselves regarding the nature of anger, feelings in others it typically engenders, and how they believe it should best be responded to.

— express and listen to varied responses of peers to questions about anger.

— contribute their ideas to formulating conclusive statements about anger.

— consider additional, deeper questions about anger and listen to information provided by the teacher/counselor.

Time needed:

45 minutes to one hour.

Materials needed:

Writing materials for each student, the five questions listed below (These should be written on individual strips or on the board in inverse order and hidden by a pulldown screen. If questions on strips are used, have tape or tacks ready for posting them one-by-one on a bulletin board.), and at least five large, blank paper strips for each task groups' written responses to the questions. (It's a good idea to provide extras.)

Directions:

1. Briefly review what the students did and what they learned in the prior activities in this unit. Emphasize: *We are finding out some very important things about anger — situations that are likely to cause angry reactions, what anger looks and feels like, and how there are different levels, or types, or anger.*

2. Ask the students to take out writing materials for some brief notes they will write to themselves to five questions about anger. Then provide a brief overview of the activity so they will know what to expect.

3. One by one present the questions on strips of paper or written on the board. It is important for the students to focus on their personal response to each question separately before considering the next one. Pause between questions for the students to write their individual notes. Explain: *You can write anything you want that will help you think of your own best, most honest and sensible answer. Your papers will not be collected and you don't have to show anyone what you have written unless you want to.*

The Questions:

1. Who has a right to get angry?

2. How are people the same and different about anger?

3. What kinds of feelings do people have when other people get angry?

4. What are some poor, unreasonable, and hurtful ways for a person to respond to a situation that makes him or her angry?

5. What are some healthy, reasonable ways for a person to respond to a situation that makes him or her angry?

4. Assist the students to form task groups of no more than four members per group. (You may wish to use existing cooperative learning groups, or formulate new ones. If this latter course is taken, guide them through a process of determining roles: leader, recorder, process consultant, encourager, etc.)

5. Give the task groups their strips of paper and magic markers. Explain: *First, your leader will ask everyone to focus their attention on the first question and ask for ideas from the group. The leader will make sure everyone who wants to speak has a chance and that everyone listens respectfully to each speaker. Then your group will work together to form a one-sentence answer to the question and the recorder will write it on the paper strip big enough so it can be seen from across the room.*

6. Circulate as the task groups hold their discussions, but be careful not to over-involve yourself in a discussion. Only make inputs if necessary to spark or "unstick" a group's discussion. At five minute intervals let everyone know how much time is remaining so they will be sure to complete their statements for all five questions.

7. Guide the culminating discussion. Restate question one. Then ask for each task group to have their recorder stand and read their conclusion. As appropriate, ask additional questions and make explanatory statements. (See "Discussion Leads," below.) Collect the strips with their responses and post them under each question or have members of the groups do this as the class observes. Since different groups will answer differently, the collection will likely provide a comprehensive response to each question. After Question One has been fully discussed, restate Question Two and follow the same procedure. Continue in this manner until all five questions have been fully discussed.

Discussion Leads

- To Question One: It is likely most or all groups will write: "Everyone has a right to get angry." Listen to all responses, then ask:

Does this mean even you have the right to become angry too? For students who are confused by their own anger or believe their anger is unacceptable, this question and its answer underscore that they are normal and acceptable when experiencing anger. Also ask:

What about other people? And:

What about other people if they get angry at you? Make sure the consensus remains that everyone has the right to be angry — even when the target is oneself. This helps students take another's perspective and realize that everyone provokes others at times and those others have the right to feel angry as a result.

- To Question Two: This is a challenging question: The fullest answer is: "People are the same in that we all become angry at times, however different things make each of us angry and we experience different types, or levels, of anger at the same things."

Help the students to understand each facet of this answer. Some groups will probably have some parts of it and others will have other parts of it. As necessary ask additional questions to bring all facets to the surface. It is important that students understand this complete response because it underscores that anger is a common, normal emotion and not bad or unacceptable in

itself, while at the same time emphasizing the reality of individual differences in our responses to varied vexations.

- To Question Three: A variety of responses may be reported to this question and all should be accepted. A most likely frequent response will be: "People get scared when other people get angry." Ask:

What makes angry people scary? Discuss how an angry person can be frightening because often they seem to gain physical strength and power, and appear to be ready to fight. Not only that they often appear to have lost the ability to think sensibly. At worst they seem about to become, or have already become, violent and "crazy." Explain:

Frequently when we get angry or scared a chemical called 'adrenalin' is released in our bodies giving us a tremendous burst of strength so that we can do something to protect ourselves without having to stop and think it over. This happens in situations where you are in immediate danger and your instincts take over like if a car is headed toward you and you have to dive out of the way, or if a dog has entered your yard and you want to scare him off. This helps us now and then, but how often do you have to dive out of the way of an oncoming car or try to scare off a dog? The fact is that thousands of years ago human beings needed that adrenalin when they faced many more terrible dangers than we do today, but we still produce that adrenalin when we get frightened and angry. When this happens it can make angry people scary.

- To Question Four: The students will probably name examples of physically and psychologically violent behaviors such as hitting, fighting, yelling, and calling names. There are two other correct responses, but first ask,

  Is the anger itself bad, or dangerous, or hurtful? Discuss how the feeling of anger is one thing and the behavior is another. Then ask:

  What if a person is really hurt unfairly by another person or a situation and makes himself/herself believe that he/she didn't feel a thing. Is that a healthy response? Discuss how denying real feelings is not healthy. When we don't allow ourselves to experience our feelings they don't really go away. They remain inside. In the case of anger they remain hidden until something happens that causes the anger to burst out. Then the person is really out of control and liable to do some damage usually to himself or herself. Then ask:

  Suppose the same thing — a person is really hurt unfairly but this time he or she knows it and feels it but doesn't express or show the anger right then. Is that healthy? Discuss how in many situations it is the smart thing to do. But once again, if expression happens too much later it may be unhealthy — blown out of proportion or unfairly directed at someone or something other than the real cause of the anger.

- To Question Five: Listen and accept all responses. Then ask these questions and provide examples if necessary. Listen to, and accept all answers:

  What about admitting to yourself that you are angry and then telling the person who caused it what you are feeling, and why, in a normal voice?

  What if someone is angry because of something you did and they tell you in a normal voice. What is your best response?

8. Conclude with remarks underscoring the understanding that in most situations in life we can talk about our feelings as well as what we need and want. Explain: *If we care for ourselves and others and if we accept and respect our own feelings and theirs, too — even angry feelings — talking things over honestly will usually improve the relationship, not hurt it. This takes courage but often it works well. In our next two activities we will help teach each other more about when and how to do this.*

9. Post the strips with the task groups' statements on the bulletin board under the questions. These may be reviewed formally and informally from time to time by individuals or the class as a whole.

Extension for Middle and High School Biology and Psychology:

Increase the challenge of this activity by assigning research into the functioning of the human brain — the role of the "old brain" in generating anger, and the role of the neocortex which allows for the application of rational thought to anger producing situations.

RATE THE REACTION
Teacher/Counselor Presentation, Scenarios, Triads and Class Discussion — A Fundamental Activity

The purpose of this activity is to reinforce learning what kinds of behavior in response to angry feelings are emotionally mature (healthy and productive) and what kinds of behaviors are emotionally immature (unhealthy and unproductive). The students are also enabled to see how the feeling of anger when combined with rational thought can be channeled in beneficial ways and become useful, or when feelings of anger are not combined with rational thought destructive actions are the likely result.

Description:

After a brief presentation regarding "The Circular Character of Anger,"* the students listen to four scenarios in which someone feels anger and then acts on the feelings. The students then discuss their reactions followed by a chance to state their "rating" of the behavior for the class.

Objectives:

Students will:

— listen to information regarding "The Circular Character of Anger."

— discuss and evaluate the actions of individuals who felt angry in four scenarios.

— express, and listen to, the evaluations of others regarding the behavior of the angry individuals in the four scenarios.

— Consider how thoughts, decisions, and self-talk can affect the behavior of a person who is experiencing anger.

Time needed:

30 to 45 minutes

Materials needed:

The diagram on the following page reproduced on chalkboard or chart:

Directions:

1. Begin by asking the class: *What are some of the most important things you have learned so far about anger?* Listen to the points the students bring up and acknowledge them for their contributions. Add your own comments as well.

2. Direct the student's attention to the diagram and explain: *Today we're going to start off by examining what actually goes on when anger occurs and what happens before and after that. We'll use this diagram to help us understand it as completely as possible.* Use the following presentation notes:

PRESENTATION: THE CIRCULAR CHARACTER OF ANGER

A. Begin by pointing to the circle and explaining that it represents what goes on within you. It includes everything except the "EVENT OR SITUATION" which occurs outside of you.

THE CIRCULAR CHARACTER OF ANGER*

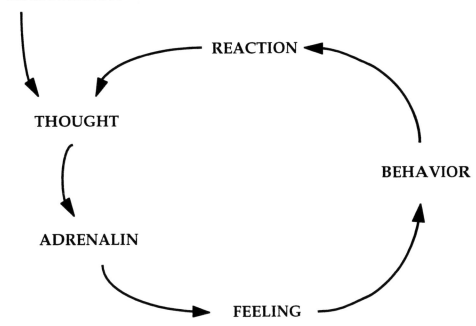

EVENT OR SITUATION

REACTION

THOUGHT

BEHAVIOR

ADRENALIN

FEELING

B. The "EVENT OR SITUATION" is what causes you to have a "THOUGHT" which may take only a split second. It's when you tell yourself what the "EVENT OR SITUATION" is. For example, let's say you are at a shopping center and a person runs into you. The person running into you is the "EVENT OR SITUATION" and then your brain tells you, "That person just ran into me."

C. This makes your brain respond by signaling your body to produce a "CHEMICAL:" adrenalin.

D. The adrenalin causes you to experience a "FEELING" in your body. Probably for most people this would be shock and some form of anger. The angry feeling might be insult or aggravation.

E. "BEHAVIOR" follows next. You do something. You can take some time to decide what to do or just react on impulse without thinking about your actions.

F. But things don't stop there. Your behavior causes a "REACTION" too. It can cause you to have a "REACTION" — thoughts and feelings — to your own behavior. And the person who ran into you has a "REACTION" of feelings and thoughts and maybe more behavior to your reaction. And if other people are around they are probably having "REACTIONS" too, and so on.

G. These "REACTIONS" become more new "EVENTS AND SITUATIONS" and the Circular Character of Anger continues to go around until someone or something stops it.

3. Ask the students: *Have you heard about something like this leading to a big fight where people got seriously hurt?* They are bound to answer, yes. Without listening to examples, ask: *At what point can the person who gets run into keep the situation from becoming a bad one?*

4. Guide the discussion to focus on the power of the person's ability to think and decide. Explain: *If the offender apologizes, it can be accepted and both parties can move on. If the offender doesn't apologize the person, feeling rightfully offended, can say, 'Hey, that hurt!' and wait to see what happens next. In the worst case where the offender blames the person for getting in his/her way, the person can keep moving and let off steam later with some physical activity or resolve firmly never to act in a similar way to anyone else. The person's ability to stop and think tell him/her that these behaviors are better than getting hurt in a fight, even though the urge to lash out at the offender who didn't apologize may have been great.*

5. Assist the students to form triads and explain: *I'm going to read you a scenario. When I've finished you will have a few minutes to discuss it with your partners. Your task is to rate or evaluate the action, or behavior, taken by a person in a situation that causes him/her to feel angry.*

6. Read the first scenario, provide time for discussion in the triads, then ask for ratings from the triads. Last, ask the questions provided at the end of the scenario for general discussion. Continue this process until all four of the scenarios have been discussed.

Scenario One

Ray, a junior in high school, and his Uncle Tim who is twenty six, always liked each other and hung out together. Ray never knew why or thought much about it, but Tim was constantly getting into fights.

One evening Ray and one of his friends, Herb, needed to go to the store and borrowed Tim's new car. Just after they pulled into the store's parking lot and were getting out of the car another car pulled in. A man got out of the car and opened his door right into the side of Uncle Tim's new car. A loud crunch was heard which caused Ray and Herb to look back. As soon as he saw what happened Ray yelled, "Hey, man, you just dinged my car, you _____, _____, _____!"

He raced over to grab the man, but the fellow ducked around his car door and ran into the store. Ray took off after him and so did Herb who could hardly believe what was happening. When Ray caught up with the man in the store he yelled even louder, hit and kicked. It took the manager and two cashiers to pull Ray away. Herb watched as another cashier called the police. That night Ray spent the night in jail. No one ever heard what happened to the other man.

How would you rate Ray's actions in response to his anger?

After the triads have reported, ask these questions for general discussion:

— *Ray's Uncle Tim wasn't there, but in what ways might he have had an influence on Ray?* (Ray liked, and looked up to, his uncle who was always getting into fights. Ray never stopped to evaluate his uncle's behavior. He was probably just doing what Tim would have done.)

— *Could Ray's anger have been useful?* (Yes, it could have spurred him to get the man's name, phone number and license number or, if necessary, to call the police on behalf of his Uncle Tim.)

— *What kinds of thoughts did Ray have that were unhelpful?* (Ray didn't think sensibly at all. He allowed his anger to rule his behavior.)

— *What sorts of thoughts or decisions might Ray have had that would have kept him out of jail that night?* ("The best thing for me to do is talk to this man and get the information Tim is going to need to get the car fixed and paid for by the man or the man's insurance company.")

Scenario Two

Diane is in the ninth grade. She's short for her age and looks much younger. Most people think she's really cute, but they assume she's only about eleven or twelve years old. A girl in Diane's school enjoys teasing her. She's constantly calling her "child," "the shrimp," and other names that are worse. Sometimes she yanks on Diane's ponytail and once she cackled, "I'm going to cut off your horsey tail. It's too big for you." Whenever these things happen Diane just giggles nervously and makes herself forget.

One afternoon when Diane got home after a bad day of being tormented at school, her younger sister, Angie, was playing "dress up" with a friend. Both little girls are in the first grade. They had out some of their mother's old clothes, jewelry and shoes. Angie held up a pair of high heels and said, "Diane, why don't you put these on? They'll make you look taller!"

At that point Diane shocked Angie and her friend, and even herself. "Why don't you mind your own business you useless, idiotic little twerp?" she screamed and stomped off to her room in tears.

How would you rate Diane's actions in response to her anger?

After the triads have reported, ask these questions for general discussion:

— *Why did Diane lash out at Angie?* (Diane displaced the anger onto her little sister that she actually felt toward the girl who constantly teased her at school.)

— *Why was Diane just as surprised as Angie when she lashed out?* (Diane repressed — hid from herself — the angry feelings she had when she was teased by the girl at school.)

— *By hiding her feelings from herself Diane deprived herself of something that may have helped. What was it?* (Diane deprived herself of thinking about the situation. Thinking may have helped her decide on actions that would have been more honorable than lashing out at Angie.)

— *What action might Diane have chosen that may have helped her?* (It might work for Diane to jokingly respond to the girl at school by saying something like, "Yeah I'm short. Could you give me a break?")

Scenario Three

Felipe is a junior in high school and a good student. He has a full life: classes, track, a social club and a girlfriend, Sonia. One of his favorite classes is journalism which he takes very seriously. Sonia is in the same class.

One Monday Felipe was unpleasantly surprised when his journalism teacher asked for the homework he had assigned on the Friday before.

"What homework?" Felipe asked. "You never assigned any homework on Friday! I was here and you didn't!"

"Yes, I did. Seems you weren't paying attention," responded the teacher.

"That's not true. You never gave us any homework," exclaimed Felipe, but then he saw the other students, including Sonia, handing in their papers. He was confused and frustrated especially when Sonia just smiled at him and that's when he really got mad.

Felipe felt a rush of heat come over his body and his mind went blank but he didn't say anything else. For the rest of the class period he didn't look at or speak to anyone. As he left class Sonia tried to talk to Felipe but he ignored her and kept walking. That annoyed her and hurt her feelings.

On his way down the hall Felipe started to talk to himself about how mad he felt. He decided to get out on the track as soon as school was over because he had noticed before how running usually took away his angry energy whenever he was feeling this way. After Felipe ran the

track a couple of times he realized something: "I must have missed that assignment because I came to class late last Friday. I'll go see the teacher tomorrow and apologize for arguing with him. I know he likes me and he'll probably let me turn the assignment in late." Then, after two more times around the track he thought about Sonia. "I'd better call her and see why she was laughing at me," he told himself.

That evening Felipe called Sonia. After saying hello he realized she was mad too and he asked her why.

"You wouldn't talk to me. You were mad because you missed that assignment but it wasn't my fault," she said.

"Well, you laughed at me. How did you expect me to feel?" Felipe retorted.

"Oh!" said Sonia. "Well, I did think it was kind of funny at the time. You hardly ever goof up like that and you were so upset. But I didn't want you to get mad at me. I'm sorry."

Felipe laughed. "Forget it. I'm not mad anymore, are you?"

"No," said Sonia. "Hey, you want to come over?"

How would you rate both Felipe's and Sonia's actions in response to their anger?

After the triads have reported, ask these questions for general discussion:

— *What did Felipe do after journalism class to help him calm down so he could think?* (Felipe exerted physical energy on the track. Physical exercise is a very effective way to dissipate angry energy.)

— What thoughts were of help to Felipe and how did they help? (Felipe decided to run on the track. Then he was able to figure out how he missed the assignment and how to try to make it up. He also realized that he'd better talk with Sonia.)

— In what ways did Felipe show confidence and courage? (Felipe encouraged himself to talk to his teacher and to Sonia. He was confident his teacher liked him and would let him make up the assignment.)

Scenario Four

Jane is a sixth grader who goes to a middle school that has a music club she really wants to join. Most of the members are in the eighth and ninth grades. In order to be selected, however, Jane has to have much better grades and be recommended, in writing, by at least two teachers.

When Jane found this out, she was very discouraged and angry. She thought it just wasn't right or fair to keep kids with average grades like her out. The next day she talked with one of her friends, Sue, who was having the same feelings about it. "Let's just forget it. The rules are stupid." Sue said, "You and I don't have a chance."

But later that week, Jane made a decision to try her best. It took time. She paid better attention in class, always did her homework, got help from her Mom and older brother when she got stuck on hard assignments and as a result her grades went up. But then Jane had to get those recommendations. Just the thought of going to two teachers and asking for letters of recommendation made her feel like giving up. Was it shyness? Fear? Or maybe the idea that she was being a goody goody? Whatever it was, she held back for days.

But then Jane made the move. What got her to do it? The anger! She reminded herself of how mad she felt about having to do all these things and that gave her the energy and courage she needed. The next day she asked her teacher if she could talk with him in private. The teacher said, "Sure. Let's talk at recess." So they did, and he said he'd be happy to write her a letter of recommendation.

Then Jane realized: "I can show the letter to Mrs. Greenway," another teacher who smiled at Jane a few times. "She's friends with my teacher." The plan worked and worked well! It took two more weeks but at the next meeting of the music club Jane was selected to become a new member.

How would you rate Jane's actions in response to her anger?

After the triads have reported, ask these questions for general discussion:

— Was Jane's anger useful? (Yes, it provided the push she needed [motivation, energy and courage].)

— What thoughts, or decisions, were of help to Jane? (The decisions to try to get better grades and to approach the teachers.)

— What sorts of things did Jane probably say to herself to get her to succeed? ("I'm smart and I can do it." "I can get good grades too even if it isn't fair that I have to." "I wish I didn't have to ask him, but my teacher likes me and will probably help.")

7. Acknowledge the students for their input and explain: *In the next activity you will work with the same two partners you have now. Each triad will have time to create a scenario and act it out for the class. So start thinking of situations, but most importantly think over how a person who has become angry can use his or her thoughts to decide how to use the anger productively, or at least how to keep it from causing a destructive result.*

8. If time remains, allow the triads to begin preparations for the next activity.

Extension for Middle and High School Language Arts and Social Science:

Assign research into famous feuds in literature and movies (examples: the Montagues and Capulets in William Shakespeare's Romeo and Juliet and the feuding families in Mark Twain's Huckleberry Finn), and in history (example: the Hatfields and McCoys). The challenge to the students should be to pinpoint key turning points in the feuds and to document how destructive reaction upon reaction to real and imagined offenses resulted in escalation and ultimate tragedy.

---

*Lorraine Bilodeau, *The Anger Workbook*. Center City, Minnesota: Hazelden Educational Materials, 1992.

PUT YOUR ANGER TO GOOD USE!
Role Playing and Discussion
A Culminating Activity

Note to teachers and counselors:

This is the final activity in a series of five activities developed to assist students to understand anger as a feeling which can lead to positive or negative behavioral outcomes. It is important to conduct all of the four activities prior to this one in order to set the stage for the lessons the students will teach each other.

The purpose of this activity is to place the primary responsibility in the hands of the students for offering learning experiences to each other regarding how to actually make use of angry feelings as the basis for positive, constructive outcomes.

Description:

After a brief discussion of the nature of anger, the students are challenged to plan a role play in which one student will serve as a narrator, another will play him/herself in an anger-provoking situation and the third will play the role of the student's most rational self who will counsel the student on how to behave. Discussion will follow each enactment. The teacher/counselor leads a final discussion.

Objectives:

Students will:

— collaborate with two peers to select a situation, to plan how to present it as a

role play to the class, to make the presentation, and to ask the class for comments.

— observe role play scenarios presented by classmates and participate in discussions of what was observed and learned from each one.

Time needed:

One 50-minute class period

Materials needed:

Props at hand selected by triads

Directions:

1. Share the following analogy with the students:

Anger is a feeling that powers actions. Without direction from the brain for how to use it, anger could be like an exploding grenade going off in all directions and lacerating the one holding it and other people nearby.

If the anger is repressed and the person won't let him/herself feel it or deal with it, the anger could be like an underwater mine just waiting for one of its spikes to get touched. When it goes off, or leaks, it damages the person's insides more than it damages anyone or anything else.

However, when people are honest with themselves, and know they are angry and decide to use the anger positively, the anger can be like an amazing power tool or a laser that does a precision job.

2. Ask the students to re-form the triads they were in for the last activity. Remind them of the scenarios they examined in that activity. In two scenarios individuals used their anger to achieve positive outcomes. In the other two scenarios the individuals did not stop to think but acted blindly and impulsively.

3. Challenge the students: *In this activity you will work with your two partners to come up with a situation. It can be a real one that one of you or someone else has faced or you can make one up. You will plan how to dramatize it for the class through role play. If it is a real situation, please don't let us know who the other people were who were involved. One of you, the first character, should be a narrator to explain to the audience what is going on throughout the dramatization. The second character will play the role of him/herself facing the situation that caused the feeling of anger. And the third character is the invisible thinking part of the second character who freezes time and talks to the second character giving good advice. This third character is very wise and caring. He or she helps the second character think the situation through and gives encouragement to use the anger in a helpful, positive way. Then the second character follows the advice of the third character. This is tricky and not easy. You will have (at least ten) minutes to plan your presentation. If you need help let me know.*

4. Last, let the students know that the narrator for each triad should ask the audience some questions to be sure they understood the meaning of the presentation. You may wish to write these questions on the board for the narrator to ask the class:

— *What was the event or situation that caused the anger?*

— *How angry did (name of second character) seem to feel?*

— *How did the third character help him or her?*

— *Is there anything else the third character could have said or done to be helpful?*

5. Allow the triads to perform their dramatizations as they feel ready. As a member of the audience, model respectful observing and listening. Intervene only when absolutely necessary and lead an applause at the end of each presentation. Be sure the third character of each triad asks the discussion questions at the end of the role play presentation.

6. Acknowledge the students for their presentations. Culminate the activity by asking:

— *Why is it important to stop and think things over when you feel anger?*

— *Why is it important to say positive things to yourself, about yourself, instead of running yourself down?*

Listen to the students' responses and acknowledge them again for their fine contributions.

Someone Who Uses His/Her Anger Well
A Circle Session

Objectives:

— to allow students to examine the behaviors of individuals they admire and respect for using their anger in productive and constructive ways

— to realize that they can use these individuals as models

After setting the tone and reviewing the ground rules, introduce the topic in your own words:

We have been focusing on the subject of anger very intensively in our class recently, but we haven't talked much about actual people we know who usually use their anger in smart ways. The topic for this session is: 'Someone Who Uses His/Her Anger Well.' Do you know someone like that? Someone who always seems to land on his or her feet? The person may seem cool when he or she is really feeling angry, yet this person doesn't go to pieces, or

explode and lose it. Instead this person handles things just right and usually ends up getting what is needed without making enemies! If you decide to take a turn, tell us about the person and perhaps give us an example of how he or she used his or her anger constructively. The topic is: 'Someone Who Uses His/Her Anger Well.'

After each circle member who wishes to speak has had a chance, conduct a review to reinforce listening skills (if time allows).

Summary Discussion Questions:

— *How do most or all of us seem to feel about these people we described?*

— *Can we imitate these people?*

A Time I Used My Anger Well

A Circle Session

Objectives:

— to allow students to acknowledge themselves for managing their anger effectively

— to examine how they were able to do it.

After setting the tone and reviewing the ground rules, introduce the topic in your own words:

This is our last circle session about anger and it allows us to do something we haven't done yet. It gives us a free license to brag a bit. The topic is: 'A Time I Used My Anger Well.' Stop and think about that! Perhaps a recent situation comes to mind when you used some of the knowledge you have been gaining about managing anger in our class and as a result you handled it well. Or, this could have been something that happened awhile ago. This means that you knew you were mad but instead of blowing it you held on to yourself and said the right things to yourself which allowed you to act in a way you are proud of now. If

you decide to take a turn tell us about the situation, your feelings, what you said to yourself and what you did. Leave out the names of the other people. Again, the topic is: 'A Time I Used My Anger Well.'

After each circle member who wishes to speak has had a chance, conduct a review to reinforce listening skills (if time allows).

Summary Discussion Questions:

— How does it make you feel to know you managed, or used, your anger well?

— What were the kinds of things we said to ourselves and what sorts of decisions did we make before we did anything?

— What will you remember whenever you become angry in the future?

INFLUENCES CAN BE CHOSEN!

OVERVIEW . . .

Awareness of the influences in our lives and the realization that these influences can be examined, chosen and managed are keys to self determination and social responsibility. This unit has been designed to foster awareness in students regarding the influences of other people — individuals and groups — and the influences of media on their lives particularly with respect to how helpful or harmful those influences might be. The primary goal of this unit is to encourage students to become intentional: to examine the multitude of influences that bombard them daily and to make responsible choices regarding how, and to what extent, they will allow themselves to be influenced.

Through a variety of active processes, this instructional unit has been designed to provide learning experiences that teach the following information or "understandings" about influence:

- The vast majority of students do not believe that bullying, aggressive behavior, violence, or bringing guns and other weapons to school are acceptable.

- Shootings and other serious violence at school are not the norm despite the attention given to such tragedies by the news and general media.

- Some individuals the students spend time with by choice or necessity have a positive influence on them, and others have a negative influence because of their particular qualities, characteristics and behaviors.

- People with positive influences are typically honest, trustworthy, respectful, caring, responsible, and self controlling. They can be chosen to imitate as role models.

- People with negative influences are typically dishonest, untrustworthy, disrespectful, uncaring, irresponsible, and impulsive. They can be used as models for how not to behave.

- Children and adolescents are most easily influenced by people their same age or somewhat older. This also means that the students, themselves, influence their peers and younger children.

- There are a multitude of formal and informal groups students may belong to by choice.

- Belonging to a group and sharing its identity is a basic human need especially for older children and adolescents and is certainly a valid reason for joining a group. There are many other benefits to joining particular groups as well.

- There are costs to group membership and for some groups these costs are very severe like being forced to harm others and getting a bad reputation.

- It's best to know as much as possible about a group before deciding whether or not to join it. This is because it's hard to leave a group you have already joined when you discover that the costs are too high.

- Each individual student has to decide for him/herself whether or not to join, or remain in, a group based on the benefits and costs of membership.

- Constant, habitual TV viewing causes sensory deprivation and can affect the quality of one's life including physical well being, moods, and academic performance.

- "Intentional TV viewing" is possible; it is wise and beneficial.

- Frequent and prolonged TV viewing so bombards the viewer's brain with rapidly changing visual images that his/her powers of imagination and critical thinking are seriously undermined. These effects can have serious consequences on the developing brains of children and adolescents.

- Facets of the relationship between media influences and violence include: (1) stimulus addiction, (2) media distortion of reality, (3) the attraction of media violence, (4) causes and effects of desensitization, (5) video game addiction, (6) reactive vs. interactive games, and (7) how some media fare resembles actual combat training.

- In addition to avoiding negative influences, it is possible to identify and consciously choose numerous positive alternatives including individuals, groups, activities, work, church, books, movies, etc.

An important resource for the development of this unit and an excellent source of additional information: *Television and the Lives of Our Children: A Manual for Teachers and Parents* by Gloria DeGaetano, M.Ed., Redmond, Washington: Train of Thought Counseling, Publisher, 1993. Phone: (425) 883-1544

COOL OR NOT COOL?
"Mini-Research Project" and Class Discussion
A Fundamental Activity

The purpose of this activity is to allow students to establish a class position on violence, aggression and bullying at school. It also provides a vehicle for helping students to change the misconception many have that weapons are prevalent at school due in part to media influence. The goal is to help students understand that violence is not appreciated by their peers and it is not the norm.

Description:

Students are asked to write brief notes to themselves to a series of four questions presented orally about bullying, anger, violence, and guns at school. Then they meet in dyads to discuss their responses. Next, taking each question in turn, the teacher/counselor asks for a show of hands to collect class data, and leads a discussion about each issue. The outcome will reveal that all, or the vast majority, of the students do not approve of bullying, aggression and violence at school. It will also reveal that weapons at school are not as prevalent as they might have thought.

Objectives:

Students will:

— individually contemplate and write notes to themselves regarding how accepting or unaccepting they are of bullying, aggression, violence, and guns at school.

— express their own feelings and listen to the responses of a dyad partner and those of other class members related to these issues.

— consider the implications of collected data from the entire class on these issues.

Time needed:

20 to 30 minutes.

Materials needed:

Writing materials for each student, and chalkboard and chalk

Directions:

1. Distribute writing materials to the students or ask them to use their own writing materials for some brief notes they will write to themselves to four questions about violence at school.

2. One by one read the questions below giving the students time to write notes to themselves on each question. It is important for them to focus on their personal response to each question separately before considering the next one. Explain: *You can write anything you want. One way you might respond is to write the word, 'cool,' or the words 'not cool.'*

Questions about Violence at School

- *How would you feel about it if a student started bullying you or someone else at school?*

- *How would you feel about it if a student became physically aggressive with you or someone else at school (shouting, hitting and kicking)?*

- *How would you feel about it if a student pulled out a real gun near you and other students at school?*

- *Have you personally ever seen a student pull out a real gun at school?*

3. Direct the students to form dyads. Give them about five minutes to discuss the four questions sharing with each other their responses.

4. Discuss responses with the class. For the first question ask, *If you think that bullying is not cool, raise your hand.* Count the responses and write this sentence filling in the number of votes: ***Bullying: not cool ____ votes.*** Eliminate any attention that may be paid to students who voted "cool" by not asking for the number of votes in the "cool" category. Then state the obvious: *As you can see, all (or the vast majority) of us think that bullying is not acceptable.* Then ask, *Why not?* Allow all students who have a comment to make it.

5. Follow this exact procedure in sequence for collecting the students' responses to the next two questions about aggression and violence.

6. Last, for question four, take the reverse tack and ask, *If you have ever personally seen anyone pull out a real gun at school, raise your hand.* The number will be slim to none.

7. Ask the class: *What does this tell us?* Through discussion assist the students to understand that even though we hear about shootings and other serious violence in schools in the news, and many television movies and programs would lead one to believe that guns are prevalent in schools, this is simply not true. The vast majority of students do not value bullying, aggression, violence, guns or other weapons at school and they conduct themselves in accordance with these values.

Extensions for Middle and High School Social Studies:

Challenge the students to expand this "mini research project" based solely on the number of students in their class to a broader number including local, state and national statistics, and then to report their findings to the class. The prime task should be to obtain ratios between numbers of students in a given population to the number of violent incidents in schools.

THE QUALITIES OF INFLUENCE
Brainstorming and Discussion
A Fundamental Activity

The purpose of this activity is to cause students to consider how susceptible they are to the influence of other people especially those who are their same age or a few years older and how these influences can be positive or negative. Through brainstorming, the students examine particular qualities, characteristics and actions of those they consider to be both positive and negative influences. They also consider how they can learn from both types of individuals and be more self-determining.

Description:

Students are asked to consider the meaning and power of influence and how they are influenced by others. They brainstorm qualities and behaviors of two types of individuals: those who have a positive influence on them and those they feel have a negative influence. They then engage in a discussion to form important understandings about their power to choose how they will be influenced and by whom.

Objectives:

Students will:

— reflect on the qualities, characteristics and actions of two individuals — one with a positive influence and one with a negative influence on their lives.

— express on a voluntary basis, and listen to, qualities, characteristics and behavior of people they and others consider to be positive and negative influences.

— discuss the power and meaning of the influence people have on one another and how this awareness can allow one to make better personal choices.

Time needed:

20 to 40 minutes

Materials needed:

Chart paper and magic marker (or chalk and chalkboard) for two lists with these headings: "People Who Influence Us Positively are...," and "People Who Influence Us Negatively are...".

Directions:

1. Briefly review what the students did in the first introductory activity in this unit. Explain: *We found out that very few people think that violence, or the instruments of violence like guns at school, are acceptable even though we may have had the impression that lots of people think these are cool. We have been influenced by the news and movies and other programs on television, and the fact that whenever there has been a violent incident in a school everybody talks about it, making it seem that schools are much more dangerous places that they really are. The key word is influenced! The activity we will do today is also about influence — the influence of*

people in our lives and how much of an effect they have on us to think, feel and act like they do.

2. Point out the first chart with the title, "People Who Influence Us Positively are...." Ask: *Is there someone who comes to your mind, someone you know well who is your same age, or a few years older, who you believe is a positive influence on you in most ways? No one is perfect, but think about this person's best qualities and characteristics and the kinds of things he or she does that you are likely to adopt as your own and imitate. The person could be an adult in your family, a friend, or anyone you spend time with. Is this person honest? Can you trust him/her? Does he/she treat you and other people considerately and with respect? Does he/she care about you and other people? Is he/she a responsible person? Is he/she usually in control of him/ herself? As you figure out what his or her qualities are that make him, or her, a good influence on you just say them out loud and I will write them on the chart.*

3. When the first list has been completed, turn the attention of the students to the other list with the heading, "People Who Influence Us Negatively are..." and explain: *Now we are going to do the opposite. Think of people your age or a few years older who you believe could be a negative influence. Many of the qualities and actions of these people will be the opposite of those on our first list — qualities you would rather not have as your own. As we do this please do not say the name of the person you are thinking of. As you figure out what this person's negative qualities are and how these could be a bad influence state them and I will write them down.*

4. Acknowledge the students for their contributions. Conclude by asking

them the following questions for open discussion:
— *Do you ever find yourself acting just like these people, as if they crawled inside your body and took over?*
— *Do you have any control over how much you act like these people?*
— *What about the people with the negative qualities? Is there anything we can learn from them?*
— *Why did I ask you to think about people your same age or a few years older? Do they have the most influence?*

Guide this discussion to bring out these understandings:

(1) everyone is influenced by other people who are both positive and negative models — children and adolescents are particularly easily influenced;

(2) we can take control to some extent when we are aware that we are being influenced — we can start to choose which people will influence us and in what ways;

(3) we can stop ourselves from acting like the people with negative influences and decide to learn how not to act from them;

(4) people are most influenced by others who are their same age or somewhat older. This means that the students are an influence on their peers and children younger than themselves!

Language Arts Extension, Elementary Grades:

Assign a writing assignment: a letter to the persons the students thought about when they brainstormed the first list to thank them for their positive qualities and for being a good influence. The letters may, or may not, be delivered by the students.

Someone Older than Me Who I Purposely Imitate
A Circle Session

Objective:

— to reinforce the understanding that there are benefits in consciously using people one respects as role models.

After setting the tone and reviewing the ground rules, introduce the topic in your own words:

Our topic for this circle session is: 'Someone Older than Me Who I Purposely Imitate.' We've been focusing on the qualities and characteristics of people and their influence on us recently. We can be influenced in many ways both by people we know personally and people we don't know personally such as characters we read about in literature or observe in movies. Famous people who are in the news might also influence us in various ways both positively and negatively. Think about someone who is older than you who you know personally, or know of — someone you admire and respect that you would like to be like in some ways so you use him or her as a role model. If you decide to speak in this session, tell us who you are thinking of if you wish, and describe his or her particular qualities and characteristics that you believe are worth adopting or imitating. The topic is: 'Someone Older than Me Who I Purposely Imitate.'

After each circle member who wishes to speak has had a chance, conduct a review to reinforce listening skills (if time allows).

Summary Discussion Questions:

— Did you notice any similarities in the people we described, and if so, what were they?

— Did anyone mention some qualities and characteristics worth imitating that you hadn't thought of?

— Is it a good idea to know you are using someone as a role model?

A Person My Age I Value As a Friend
A Circle Session

Objective:

— to assist students to value friendship and consider the influence friends have on one another.

After setting the tone and reviewing the ground rules, introduce the topic in your own words:

Our topic for this circle session is: 'A Person My Age I Value as a Friend.' In our class we have been concerned with how people influence one another and everyone is subject to being influenced. We can even be influenced by people we don't even know personally in positive or negative ways who we read about or observe in movies or the news. However, one of the strongest influences in our lives is from people we associate with because we like them and they are very important to us — our friends. You can certainly have friends who are much older and younger than you are, but for most people their friends are about their same age. Who comes to mind for you? If you take a turn tell us the name of your friend if you want and describe his or her positive qualities and characteristics. The topic is: 'A Person My Age I Value as a Friend.'

After each circle member who wishes to speak has had a chance, conduct a review to reinforce listening skills (if time allows).

Summary Discussion Questions:

— *Did you notice any similarities in the qualities and characteristics of the friends we described and if so what were they?*

— *In what ways do friends influence each other?*

— *Is it a good idea to know how your friends influence you and vice versa?*

WHAT DOES IT COST TO BELONG?

Task Groups and Discussion
A Fundamental Activity

The purpose of this activity is to assist students to increase their understanding of how group membership operates. The human need for belonging is validated along with understanding of the benefits of belonging to any group. This activity also allows students to examine possible negative costs of group membership. Finally, students are challenged to carefully consider the costs before becoming identified with, or remaining with, a group.

Description:

After a brief review of the former activity regarding the influence of individuals, the students are asked to form task groups in order to take a look at the influence of groups. In these groups they undertake three tasks by listing: (1) existing formal and nonformal groups they might join or already belong to; (2) the reasons people their age would join or remain a member; and (3) the costs of belonging. A structured class discussion occurs after each list is generated and shared with the class. A final point is made regarding the student's power to make a personal choice based on benefits and costs.

Objectives:

Students will:

— assist task group members to generate lists of factors regarding group membership.

— express and listen to varied responses of peers to questions about the benefits and costs of group membership.

— consider their personal power to make choices regarding which groups they might join or continue to belong to, based on the benefits and costs of membership.

Time needed:

40 to 50 minutes

Materials needed:

Writing materials for each task group and chalkboard

Directions:

1. Briefly review what the students did and what they learned in the prior activities in this unit. Emphasize: *We are focusing on how easily people are influenced and that you don't have to be automatically programmed like a computer by these influences. Everyone has choices but first you have to be aware of what the influences are before you can decide to accept or reject them. In our last activity we looked at the influence of individual people in our lives. Today we will take a look at how groups influence their members.*

2. Assist the students to form task groups of no more than four members per group. (You may wish to use existing cooperative learning groups, or formulate new ones. If this latter course is

taken guide them through a process of determining roles: leader, recorder, process consultant, encourager, etc.)

3. Explain the overall plan for the activity: they will have three tasks, each taking five minutes, to generate three group lists. After each list has been generated the recorder from each group will read his/her group's list to the class. Then the class will discuss the information before moving on to the next task.

4. State the first task: *As a group make a list of all the groups you know of that people your age are members of, or could join. In some cases you have to be chosen and invited to join and in other cases anyone could join by their own choice. Either way, list them. The groups you list could be teams, associations or clubs here at school; they could be church groups, or even the kind of club that the people formed themselves like (name a couple of local informal groups or gangs they will recognize). You might know of some groups for people your age in the community. Be sure to list them too.*

5. Ask the recorders in each group to read their groups' lists aloud. As the lists are read chart the names of the groups. As repetition occurs make check marks by the name of each group to show these repetitions.

6. Discuss the charted class list. Ask:

— *Did you expect this list to be so long?* (Point out that if they are looking for a group to belong to, they might not have thought of some of those listed.)

— *Which of these groups are by invitation only?* (Place an asterisk by the ones named.)

— *Does it make a group better just because you have to be invited to join?* (Discuss how some people think this is true but doesn't have to be.)

7. State the second task: *Think about why people your age might join a group. What are the main benefits of being a member. List as many as you can think of.*

8. Ask the recorders to read their lists as everyone listens.

9. Discuss the benefits:

— *If you join a group mainly because you just want to belong is that okay?* (Point out that belonging to a group and sharing its identity is a basic human need especially for people their age and is certainly a valid reason for joining a group.)

10. State the third task: *Now, think of every negative you can. What are the costs of group membership? Some of the costs are the same for any group like having to show up when they expect you, but many of the costs are particular to specific groups. For example, if you belong to an art association the art materials might be expensive. Or there might be some influence on you in some groups that you know would not be good for you or your reputation. As you generate your list of negatives it's not necessary to name the group (or its leader) that might have those costs.*

11. Ask the recorders to read their lists of costs of group membership as everyone listens. Encourage them not to name the groups or their leaders. (This is for their own safety.)

12. Discuss the costs:

— *Which costs are the most severe?* (If no one mentions "being forced to do harmful things to other people" and "getting a bad reputation because you are a member of that group" mention them yourself.)

— *Why is it good to know as much as possible about a group before you join it?* (Point out that even if you are already a member of a group and find out later that the costs are more than you want to "pay" you still have a choice about whether or not to remain. It's just harder to quit than not to join in the first place.)

13. Culminate by sharing a couple of personal experiences you had when you were the age of your students perhaps with two different groups — one that had a positive influence on you and one that you decided not to join or left because the costs were too high. Summarize:

— *Everyone needs to belong to a group of friends that has its own identity and purpose. It's good for you but you need to realize that the group influences you and gives you a reputation. The influences and the reputation can be positive or negative. The activities of the group may be helpful or harmful to you and to other people. Only you can decide for yourself what group to join or stay with based on the benefits and costs.*

Extension for Middle and High School Social Science:

Assign the task of researching and reporting on larger organizations — their purposes, activities, influences on members, and reputations. Some possibilities: AFL/CIO, National Rifle Association, American Red Cross, Kiwanis, particular churches, Ku Klux Klan, and various governments, past and present, including their own.

A Group I Belong To and Its Benefits
A Circle Session

Objective:

— to assist students to identify the benefits of belonging to the groups (clubs, teams, associations, etc.) they belong to or might join.

After setting the tone and reviewing the ground rules, introduce the topic in your own words:

Our topic for this circle session is: 'A Group I Belong To and Its Benefits.' We've been focusing on the power of individuals to influence each other in our class. Many times that influence is multiplied when it comes to groups such as clubs, teams, associations, or just a group of friends who hang out together. Belonging to a group is important to almost everyone. It's a human need to belong to a group. No group offers everything to its members, however, but there are some that offer more than others. If you take a turn to speak in this session, tell us about a group of some form you belong to and what you like

about it and get from it. For this session we'll skip any negatives and just focus on the benefits of the groups we belong to. The topic is: 'A Group I Belong To and Its Benefits.'

After each circle member who wishes to speak has had a chance, conduct a review to reinforce listening skills (if time allows).

Summary Discussion Questions:

— *Were there any noticeable similarities in the benefits we mentioned in the groups we belong to and if so what were they?*

— *In what ways are members influenced by the groups they belong to?*

— *Why is it a good idea to know as much as you can about a group before you join it?*

A Time I Wouldn't Go Along with the Group
A Circle Session

Objectives:

— to enable students to identify types of unhealthy activities and pressures some groups place on their members

— to discuss ways to overcome these pressures.

After setting the tone and reviewing the ground rules, introduce the topic in your own words:

We have been focusing on the positives and negatives of being a member of a group. To belong is important and good for us, but sometimes the costs of belonging can outweigh the benefits. An example is when the group has decided to do something you believe is harmful in some way and they may be putting pressure on you to join in. Our topic for this circle session is: 'A Time I Wouldn't Go Along with the Group.' Can you think of a situation in which something like that happened to you, a situation you would be comfortable telling us about? It would be best not to mention names of groups or individuals in the groups, but if

you take a turn tell us how you resisted joining in. Let's take a minute to think it over. The topic is: 'A Time I Wouldn't Go Along with the Group.'

After each circle member who wishes to speak has had a chance, conduct a review to reinforce listening skills (if time allows).

Summary Discussion Questions:

— *What were the main reasons most (or all) of us resisted what the groups had decided to do?*

— *We heard several different ways to resist group pressure. Which ones seemed smart and worth trying yourself if you are in this position with a group again?*

— *It may have been difficult when these incidents happened, but how do you feel now about resisting?*

WHAT IS YOUR TV DOING TO YOU?
Activity Series, Class Survey and Discussion
A Fundamental Activity

The purpose of this activity is to assist students to understand that too much TV viewing causes sensory deprivation and can affect the quality of their lives including their physical well being, moods, and academic performance. They participate in a revealing class survey and are presented with information to help them understand that intentional TV viewing is possible; it is wise and beneficial.

Description:

This activity begins with a demonstration of the effects of too much TV viewing. A discussion ensues about how people appear and how they act after watching several hours of TV. This is followed by a teacher/counselor presentation on sensory deprivation. Next, the class engages in a survey about the relationship between the amount/type of TV viewing and academic grades. Last, the teacher/counselor once again makes a presentation about how much TV is watched by the average child and adolescent, and how they can change these habits to become "intentional viewers."

Objectives:

Students will:

— share their observations about how excessive TV viewing affects peoples' minds, bodies and moods.

— participate in a class survey by responding to questions about how much TV they watch in an average week, which shows are most frequently and infrequently watched, and what their most recent grades have been in Language Arts, Math, Social Science, and Science.

— discuss the results of the survey and the implications of those results regarding TV viewing.

— Listen to and consider some ideas and statistics regarding TV viewing and how to become an "intentional viewer."

Time needed:

One full class period of at least 50 minutes. (Large classes are likely to take two class periods due to the time invested in tallying the survey.)

Materials needed:

Enough copies of the "TV Survey" for each student, the chart (from the next page) copied onto chart paper, and a chalkboard or whiteboard:

Code name:	Total hours TV watched per week:	Type show watched most often:	Type show watched least often:	Average grade:
(one line needed per student)				

Directions:

1. Begin by explaining that this activity has two parts. The first part will be volunteering to act and speak on several different topics related to television and its effects. The second part will be a class survey.

2. Explain: *Let's have some fun with this. Pretend that you aren't here but instead you are at home watching TV and that you have been doing it for the last three hours."* (Raise your hand or an object such as a book and say: "This is the screen." The students will immediately develop a vacant eye stare at the "screen.") *Now keep the same look on your face and turn around and look at each other. What do you see?*

3. Allow each student who wishes to comment to do so. (Make sure they acknowledge the "vacant stares.") Then make the discussion more interesting by asking:

— *What have you noticed after people, including yourself, watch TV for several hours and someone else calls their name?*

— *What if someone tries to talk to them?*

— *How are their bodies affected?*

— *What is their mood — cheerful and refreshed or hyperactive and cranky?*

4. After the students have responded and laughed about how TV affects people, explain: *We've been talking about something that is actually a serious matter. It's called 'sensory deprivation' and it happens to us when we change our reality from 3D to 2D for too long a time. When this happens to people their senses except for sight and sound shut down. Sight especially becomes overstimulated because they are watching vivid, fast-moving images. This excites their central nervous systems but their bodies lose contact with the outside world. They may seem like they're vegging out and lost because sensory deprivation causes them to disconnect and become disoriented. This makes people irritable and cranky. To develop well and stay in good shape people need to use all of their senses as much of the time as possible. They also need physical activity. Watching TV doesn't allow these to happen.*

5. Conduct the survey. Distribute the "TV Survey" sheets to the students and guide them through the process of filling them in. Be sure to tell them not to write in their actual names but to use code names instead in order to give them privacy.

6. After the sheets have been handed back ask a student to read the following information on each sheet out loud as you fill it in on the chart: (1) the student's code name (to protect each student's identity); (2) total hours of TV watching per week; (3) type of show watched most often; (4) type of show watched least often; (5) the four grades. (Average the grades into one grade for the chart.)

7. After the chart has been filled in guide the students to determine what it indicates. Ask:

— *What do you notice about the TV watching habits of the students with the highest average grades?*

— *What do you notice about the TV watching habits of the students with the lowest average grades?*

— *Does this tell you anything about how much TV is too much?*

— *Does this tell you anything about what kinds of TV shows are best for you to choose and which ones are not as beneficial?*

8. Conclude the activity with the following information and ideas:

— *TV isn't all bad. When it's used wisely it can be very enjoyable, entertaining and interesting. The key word is used! We need to use it, not let it use us!*

— *The average student has spent 22,000 hours watching TV by the time he or she is eighteen years old. That's twice the time spent in classrooms and more time in any one activity other than sleeping. (This is according to Conrad Kottak in Prime-Time Society.)*

— *By the time the average person is twenty-one years old, he or she will have seen one million television commercials. (This is stated by Niel Postman in Conscientious Objections.)*

— *The average American child watches five hours per week of television commercials alone according to the AAA Foundation for Traffic Safety.*

— *Using TV wisely is called "intentional viewing" and a lot of students have learned to do it. They keep the TV off and select the shows they want to see. If the TV at home is under someone else's control they stay away from it when they choose to.*

TV SURVEY

Code Name:_____

I. How much TV do you watch each week?

Average number of hours each weekday

afternoon and evening? _____ x 5 = _____

On most Saturdays? _____

On most Sundays? _____

Total: _____

II. What types of shows and movies do you watch most and least? Choose two. Write a 1 next to the type you watch most and a 0 by the kind you watch least. You may add types that aren't listed under the word "Other."

____ Sitcoms   Other:

__ PBS/Educational programs   ___ _____

_ Action/Adventure   ___ _____

Talk shows   ___ _____

Horror   ___ _____

III. What were your most recent grades in these subjects? Write the grade beside the name of the subject.

Language Arts   ____ Social Science

Math   ____ Science

HOW DO YOU 'FEED' YOUR MIND?

Experiment, Demonstration and Discussion
A Fundamental Activity

The purpose of this activity is to help students conclude for themselves that frequent and prolonged TV viewing so bombards their brains with rapidly changing visual images that their powers of imagination and critical thinking are seriously undermined, as opposed to the effects of listening to another person speak or read, or reading to themselves, both of which promote their abilities to imagine and think critically. They also consider the effects of habitual TV viewing on their developing brains and the fact that they have ultimate control on how much TV they watch.

Description:

Student demonstrations take place comparing three different methods of consuming food — (1) in a normal, slow, relaxed, leisurely manner, (2) blindfolded and fed slowly by others, and (3) blindfolded and fed in a rapid, forced manner. The food demonstration is debriefed and then the class is asked, to compare the three demonstrations of consuming food for the body to three different ways of consuming information for the mind — (1) reading to oneself, (2) listening as someone else speaks or reads, and (3) watching TV. Discussion centers on how the students reached their conclusions and the implications of those conclusions.

Objectives:

Students will:

— observe demonstrations of three different ways of consuming food.

— compare the demonstrations of three different ways to consume food for the body to three different ways to consume information and stories for the mind, namely reading, listening as another person speaks or reads, and watching popular TV shows, movies, and commercials.

— discuss the implications of this experiment on the development of their growing brains.

Time needed:

20 to 40 minutes

Materials needed:

About 16 ounces of three different flavors of ice cream, pudding or jello; three plates with sections (one for each flavor); three spoons; and a blindfold

Directions:

Part One: The Experiment

1. It is best not to give an overview of this activity to the class. Simply begin by telling them that they are all going to be a part of an experiment having to do with food for the body and food for the mind. Then ask for three volunteers. Select three cooperative, outgoing and well-liked students (who like the particular food you are about to serve them and are not allergic to it) and explain that they will wait outside the classroom until they are called to enter individually. Explain that after the first and second students have finished inside they will return and wait outside until all three have had their turn. Then all three will be invited back in. When they are outside they should not tell each other what they experienced when it was their turn to demonstrate inside the classroom until later.

2. Explain to the class: *You are just as important as the volunteers in this experiment because your observations are needed. You will probably not understand the purpose of the three demonstrations I'm going to do with the volunteers and that's okay. Just watch and report what you see.*

3. Bring in the first volunteer and ask him/her to be seated at a table in front of the class. Serve the student a plate with portions of the three different flavors of ice cream (or pudding, or jello), give him/her a spoon and ask him/her to start eating and not to rush but to enjoy the food. As the student eats, engage him/her in pleasant conversation. You could ask, *How to do like it? Which flavor do you like best? Can you remember another time when you ate this and enjoyed it? Tell us all about it —*

where you were, when it happened and who you were with? Ask the class to join in the conversation as well. When the student has finished, thank him/her and ask him/her: *How did you like the food and the way you got it?* Listen to his/her response and then ask him/her to leave the class and go back outside.

4. Ask the class for their observations:

— *Did he/she enjoy the experience?*

— *Did he/she eat at his/her own pace?*

— *Was he/she allowed to use his/her imagination during the experience?*

— *How did he/she seem to feel afterward?*

As a result of this discussion it should be established that the student may have been self-conscious and puzzled but enjoyed the food, went at his/her own pace, used his/her imagination, and was alert, and in a reasonably good mood afterward.

5. Ask the second student volunteer to come into the room, greet him/her and ask him/her to sit at the table. Then explain: *I'm going to blindfold you and then feed you some food. As you are fed you can tell us what you think the flavor of each bite is and how you like it, okay?* In a considerate manner, feed the student each spoonful after each one has been completely chewed and swallowed. As you feed the student ask him/her questions about what he/she imagines the flavor of each spoonful is, etc. As before with the first volunteer, ask, *Can you remember another time when you ate this and enjoyed it? Tell us all about it — where you were, when it happened and who you were with?* Invite the class to converse with the student as well. When the "feeding session" is over, thank the

student and ask him/her: *How did you like the food and the way you got it?* Listen to his/her response and then ask him/her to go back outside.

6. Ask the class for their observations by asking the same four questions from the first demonstration. The results should be the same this time as for the first demonstration: the student may have been self-conscious and puzzled but enjoyed the food, went at a reasonable pace, used his/her imagination, and was alert, and in a reasonably good mood afterward.

7. Ask the third student volunteer to enter the classroom and ask him/her to sit at the table. Give no explanations nor allow any discussion at any time during this demonstration. Put the blindfold on the student and feed him/her as rapidly as you can without letting him/her choke. This may not last long due to all of the students' surprised reactions. After about five bites, or more, take the blindfold off the student and ask him/her: *How did you like the food and the way you got it?* Another important question for this student is: *What if the feeding had gone on for an hour or more?* Listen to his/her responses and then ask the student to go back outside. At this point tell the three volunteers that they may tell each other what they experienced when it was their turn to demonstrate before coming back into the classroom in a minute or two.

8. Ask the class for their observations of the third demonstration by asking the same four questions you put to them after the first and second demonstrations. The results should confirm that the food was probably not enjoyed very much because it was served at the pace

of the server not the consumer, there was no chance for the student to imagine or discuss anything, and he/she was probably feeling overwhelmed and not in a very good mood afterward.

9. Ask the three volunteers to come back into the classroom.

Part II. Conclusions and Discussion

10. Pose the central question: *We just saw three people consume food for their bodies. Do you know what 'food' for the mind is? It's information. All of us are consuming food for our minds — information — all the time in various ways. Now, let's turn a 'mental corner' and compare these three methods of consuming food to three ways to consume information. The three ways to consume food are: (1) to feed yourself, (2) to be fed in a pleasant way, and (3) to be fed rapidly and forcefully. Three ways to consume information are: (1) to watch sitcoms and many other types of shows and movies and commercials on TV, (2) to read to yourself, and (3) to listen as someone else speaks or reads aloud in person, on the radio or on tape or CD. Which method compares with which?*

(Use the chart on the next page as a guide.)

11. Invite each student to speak who wishes to respond to the central question. When a student answers in the desired manner (as shown above) ask, *How did you know that?*

Guide the students to conclude that reading to oneself allows the mind to create images along with the information being read and to think about its meaning because it is self-paced. The reader is in control. Listening to a reader or speaker also allows the listener to use his/her imagination and to

Note: The answers are: (You may wish to write these on the chalkboard.)

To feed yourself	—	To read to yourself
To be fed in a pleasant way	—	To listen as someone else speaks or reads aloud in person, on the radio or on tape or CD
To be fed rapidly and forcefully	—	To watch sitcoms and many other types of shows and movies and commercials on TV

think about what he/she is hearing. If it's a conversation he/she can also interact with the speaker. It is usually a pleasant and refreshing experience. But after prolonged watching of shows, movies and commercials on TV most people are not refreshed because they have been bombarded with images (force-fed!) which shuts down their ability to use their imaginations and doesn't give them time to think about or evaluate what they are watching. Their bodies are held there as if hypnotized, just watching the rapid visual changes flash every few seconds on the screen.

12. Ask the students, *What does watching TV for hours and hours each day do to developing brains — the brains of children and teenagers?*

Assist them to understand that frequent and prolonged TV viewing seriously contributes to lack of development in growing brains. The brain is "plastic" and will stretch when challenged. TV viewing generally doesn't allow the brain to imagine or think which must occur for it to stretch and grow. Like the saying goes, "Use it or lose it!"

13. Finally, ask, *Who controls how much TV you watch?* Listen as the students talk about their own ultimate control but how difficult it is at times to resist watching TV.

Extension for all grades — Language Arts:

Read an engaging short story to the class and discuss it. Ask the students how they enjoyed listening, about scenes they may have imagined, and how they evaluated the actions of the characters. Point out how listening without viewing allows the mind to be active while not having the hypnotic effect that TV viewing has with its emphasis on visual overstimulation.

Middle and High School Biology:

Challenge the students to conduct research into the effects of sensory deprivation on the growth of dendrites on brain cells in young animals including human children and adolescents.

I Was Being Influenced and Didn't Realize It
A Circle Session

Objectives:

— to enable students to identify influences in their lives that heretofore have been unconscious

— to tell each other about them.

After setting the tone and reviewing the ground rules, introduce the topic in your own words:

The topic for this circle session is 'I Was Being Influenced and Didn't Realize It.' As we've been concerning ourselves in the class with the various influences in our lives that affect us both positively and negatively, have you come to realize that one or more are operating on you that you weren't aware of? The influence could be a human one and perhaps positive. Maybe there is someone you associate with a lot like a grandparent who you may have been taking for granted and suddenly you realize how lucky you are to have him or her in your life. Or the opposite may be the case. Perhaps you have been watching TV a lot and you really didn't know how doing that affects your

personality and brain. Whatever it may be, we would be interested in hearing about it. The topic is: 'I Was Being Influenced and Didn't Realize It.'

After each circle member who wishes to speak has had a chance, conduct a review to reinforce listening skills (if time allows).

Summary Discussion Questions:

— What enabled you to recently realize that you were being influenced without being aware of it?

— Did anyone mention an influence that you hadn't thought of that you now realize is one of yours?

— What's the value of knowing who and what is influencing you and in what ways?

MEDIA SMARTS!
Task Groups, Student (or Teacher/Counselor) Presentations and Discussion — A Fundamental Activity

Note to teachers and counselors:

Two activities related to media influences have preceded this one allowing students to understand the effects of frequent and prolonged TV viewing on their academic performance and growing brains. This activity culminates the series. It may be altered for grades four through six by presenting the information to the students yourself in a series of "lessons." If you are working with fourth, fifth or sixth graders and choose this option end each presentation by asking them what the information means to them. Help them understand that they do not have to be controlled by media influences. Expose them to this chant: "Turn it off or leave the room!"

The purpose of this activity is to enable the students to teach each other about key facets of the relationship between media influences and violence including: (1) stimulus addiction, (2) media distortion of reality, (3) the attraction of media violence, (4) causes and effects of desensitization, (5) video game addiction, (6) reactive vs. interactive games, and (7) how some media fare resembles actual combat training.

Description:

Part I

After a brief review of the concepts presented in the two prior activities, the students are divided into seven task groups, each having its own presentation topic and information to "teach" to the class. The balance of the class period is devoted to preparing the presentations in a creative way.

Part II

Each task group makes its presentation to the class followed by a brief teacher/counselor-led discussion. After all the presentations have been made the teacher/counselor leads a culminating discussion regarding the overall implications of the information provided by the students.

Objectives:

Students will:

— discuss a concept related to media influences with several other students in a task group and plan how to present the information to the class in a subsequent class session.

— observe, listen to, and consider concepts presented by students in other task groups.

— participate in class discussions that relate to each presentation and to a culminating discussion regarding the importance of controlling the influence of the media on oneself instead of being controlled.

Time needed:

Two class sessions: one for planning and one (perhaps two) for presentations and discussion.

Materials needed:

The seven "Information Sheets" for the task groups and materials for visual aids that some of the task groups might need.

Directions:

Part One: Presentation Planning

1. Begin by asking the class: *What are some of the most important things you have learned so far about the influence on your life of watching hours and hours of TV?* Listen to the points the students bring up and acknowledge them for their contributions. Add your own comments as well.

2. Explain: *The name of this activity is 'Media Smarts' and its purpose is to give each one of us more of them. We've been focusing on how it affects us when we spend lots of time watching TV but we haven't looked much at how we are affected by what we are watching, or playing if it's a video game. In this activity we will consider these issues. You are going to be the 'teachers.' You will be a member of a task group that will get some 'inside information' about one aspect of 'Media Smarts.' Then you will plan how to 'team teach' the information to the rest of us in a three to ten minute lesson. You will have the rest of the class period for planning. (In the next class period[s] the groups will make their presentations.)*

3. Assist the students to form the seven task groups. (Ideal size would be no more than four members per group.)

An alternative: Form 14 groups, two per presentation topic.

4. Distribute the seven "Information Sheets," one per group. Suggest: *Read the information and discuss it among yourselves. Then plan an interesting way to teach it to us. Be creative. You might want to make some visual aids or use the chalkboard. You could put on a short dramatization or role play. You might have a short story to tell that would help to make one or two of your points. Please let me know if you need some input from me.* Circulate as the groups discuss the information and begin planning their presentations serving as a consultant as needed.

Part Two: Presentations and Discussion

5. Call on each task group to make its presentation in the order given below. Model attentive listening skills and lead an applause at the end of each presentation. After each one, lead a short discussion by asking the class:

— *How do you react to this information?*

— *What was the most significant point for you?*

— *What questions do you have for the presenters?*

The titles of the seven presentations are:

    I.   What is Stimulus Addiction?

    II. How the Media Distorts Our View of Reality

    III. Why are Many People Attracted to Watching Violence?

    IV. What is Desensitization?

V. Why do Some People Become Addicted to Video Games and What Happens to Them?

VI. What's the Difference Between a Reactive and an Interactive Game?

VII. Who's Being Trained to Kill?

6. Culminate with a summary discussion. Ask the class:

— *In all the presentations what information was the most interesting for you?*

— *Why do you think this activity is called, 'Media Smarts?'*

— *In what ways do you plan to use some of the 'media smarts' you may have gained from this activity?*

Listen to all of the comments students make and make your own in response to the questions. Guide the discussion toward the concept that each person has a choice to use the media intelligently or to be its tool.

What is Stimulus Addiction?

Information Sheet #1

A brain researcher, Paul Gathercoal, says that for many people watching TV may become habit-forming and addicting. He explains that:

- Stimulus addiction releases chemicals that are already in the body (endorphins) instead of putting new chemicals in the body as happens with drug addiction.

- The endorphins are released when the person becomes stressed or has a strong feeling. The right amount of endorphins is released each day as a person does normal things like going to school and talking with other people.

- Media (TV, video and computer games, etc.) often overstimulate the flow of endorphins by causing people to pay very close attention to the exciting things they are seeing and to have strong feelings.

- When this happens constantly for a long time two things happen to us: First we can become addicted to the hyped excitement and the endorphins it releases in our bodies. We just have to have our daily fix of war movies, cartoons, horror, etc. And it takes more and more endorphins to make us feel satisfied so we keep watching. Second, we burn out on all the media excitement and become dull people who can't respond to real situations with real people in normal and appropriate ways.

- It happens! Children and teenagers are the most susceptible to stimulus addiction. But even adults can become television addicts.

How the Media Distorts Our View of Reality

Information Sheet #2

- The media is constantly trying to tell us what's happening, how to act, how to dress, what to eat and drink — what's hot and what's not! Are some people being influenced and allowing themselves to be controlled?

- The news tells us about unusual events — tragedies and anything that's out of the ordinary. After watching the news it's easy to forget that for every item about something that went wrong millions of ordinary events occurred in people's lives that went right. Yet many people start to think of the tragedies as being ordinary and talk about them as if they happened far more often than they do. Guns in schools are an example. Yes, there is more violence in schools across the nation reported by the news. This is because there are more people and more schools and it makes a "good news story" but violence in schools is still very rare and not normal. And no one likes it.

- Imagine that someone in your school does something very unusual. Wouldn't everyone hear about it that same day? And wouldn't it be likely that people outside the school who heard about it would talk about how "things like that happen all the time at that school?"

- Do sitcoms, soap operas and MTV influence us? Think about how many people imitate the remarks the actors make, the clothes they wear, and the way they act.

- What about sexuality? Is real, honest and healthy sexuality usually shown? The shows often show sexuality as cold and uncaring or a dishonest way to manipulate or take advantage of someone. When it comes to the commercials, sexuality is used to sell practically anything you can think of.

Why are Many People Attracted to Watching Violence?

Information Sheet #3

- It's human nature to pay attention to a dramatic event. In fact, if human beings did not have the instinct to focus immediately on sudden movement, noise, anything that stimulates our senses, we could not survive. It's how we know about danger and prepare ourselves to deal with it. In that way we are just like all other animals.

- Any form of violence is particularly bound to get the attention of any person even artificial violence like the kind we see acted out on TV. Our basic instincts do not immediately tell us, "Oh, that's on TV. It's not a threat to me." We just watch — usually fascinated. It's normal for human beings to do that.

- But too much of it is not good for us. There are serious consequences to watching lots of violence, even cartoon violence, on TV. In her book, *Television and the Lives of Our Children*, Gloria de Gaetano tells us that most children and teenagers won't become criminals because they watched hundreds of violent images daily for years. But, she explains, they are likely to develop one or more of these characteristics:

  — increased aggressive behavior

  — more likely to use violence and physical force to try to solve their problems

  — more inclined to see the world as a dangerous place and become fearful of their surroundings

  — more likely to react without thinking and more ready to fight when something happens

  — less likely to be cooperative

  — less likely to want to negotiate or work things out with others

  — more likely to be habituated (addicted) to "pseudo-excitement"

What is Desensitization?

Information Sheet #4

- *Webster's New World Dictionary* tells us that "desensitize" means to take away the sensitivity of; make less sensitive ... to make (a person, animal ...) nonreactive... In other words, desensitization is a process that makes people less able to use their five senses of sight, hearing, touch, taste and smell, and less able to react to things they would normally react to.

- Sometimes a person may be oversensitive in some way like being abnormally afraid of a certain animal or insect. In situations like this counselors can use the process of desensitization to help the person by putting the thing they fear near them again and again closer each time until the person realizes that no harm will come to him or her and the fear goes away.

- But in other situations it is not valuable or helpful to become desensitized. One of the effects of watching hours and hours of violence in the media is that a person can become desensitized to real life violence and human suffering. People who watch a lot of TV violence are not as likely to feel normal alarm and sadness when other people have been hurt or killed by an actual criminal or in a real accident. They are less likely to be compassionate and feel sorry for victims.

- Is there a danger to our society if too many people have become desensitized to real violence? What if you are the victim and other people are nearby but have become desensitized to real violence and the pain of victims?

Why do Some People Become Addicted to Video Games and What Happens to Them?

Information Sheet #5

Video games are exciting and many players can hardly break away from them. For many people the more they play the more they want to keep playing. They have become video game addicts.

In a book called, *Endangered Minds: Why Our Children Don't Think*, Jane Healy explains why video games are so enticing:

- They give feelings of control and mastery to the players. Everyone likes feeling powerful and in control of something.

- By playing and practicing more the level of difficulty is raised. The challenges are continually there and that is exciting.

- There are immediate and continual rewards. You always know exactly where you stand. This is also called "reinforcement" and it causes people to keep playing the game.

- By playing the game you get to escape from the real world where people and relationships are unpredictable and sometimes unpleasant. The games are predictable and do not make the player adjust to changing feelings like people do.

- The games can be lots of fun but they don't allow the player to use and develop important ways of using their brains. These ways of thinking are: finding meaning, reflecting, planning, creating, designing, and problem solving of real problems. Not only that, video games do not allow the player to use his or her whole body, or to relate to other people to develop social skills. If too many hours are spent playing video games these important brain functions are not being used enough and a person grows up handicapped.

In her book, *The Second Self: Computers and the Human Spirit*, Sherry Turkle points out: "When you play a video game you enter into the world of the programmer who made it."

What's the Difference Between a Reactive and an Interactive Game?

Information Sheet #6

- Many video games and many computer games are reactive. *Street Fighter II* and *Mario Brothers* are examples. Games like *See the USA* and *Carmen Sandiego* are interactive. They have been designed to allow the player to use and develop many important brain functions while having fun at the same time.

- In her book *Television and the Lives of Our Children*, Gloria de Gaetano points out the differences between reactive games and interactive games:

  — The player learns to expect problems to be solved in an instant without real personal involvement in reactive games. But in interactive games the player learns what it takes to solve real problems: patience, trying things, keeping at it, being cool, and being flexible.

  — In a reactive game experiences are constantly given to the player. However, in an interactive game the player has to gather information in order to make the right choice.

  — The player learns that choices are limited in a reactive game — usually there's only one right action. But the player in an interactive game learns to seek lots of ways to succeed.

  — In a reactive game the player learns to see problems as right or wrong. Reactive games also teach the player that the best way to solve a problem is to get rid of what's causing it. An interactive game is the opposite. The player learns to solve problems in many useful ways like predicting what will happen, planning and organizing, experimenting with possible solutions, and evaluating to see if those solutions worked.

  — The player in a reactive game learns to use instinctive, reactive behavior to respond to a problem. But in an interactive game the player learns to think about all of the parts of a problem and finds out that what might work in one case may not work in other cases.

  — In a reactive game the player learns to forget about using his or her own imagination and how it could help in solving a problem. But in an interactive game the player learns to use his or her imagination to get good ideas.

  — The player in a reactive game learns to place him or herself in the programmer's reality. The interactive game player learns to use his or her own thoughts and imagination to co-create his or her own reality.

Who's Being Trained to Kill?

Information Sheet #7

- *On Killing* is the name of a book written in 1995 by Dave Grossman who is a Lieutenant Colonel and a psychologist in the U.S. Army. The book has received a lot of attention and many thousands of copies have been sold. The author makes some very interesting and shocking points.

- First, he explains that all animals including human beings find it very difficult to kill a member of their own species. Even in self defense it is hard for many humans to kill a human attacker. It is true that in World War II only 15 to 25 percent of the soldiers were willing to fire their rifles in combat.

- After that the Army got better at training soldiers to overcome their instinct not to kill by using a process called "conditioning." One way this is done is to make the enemy seem less human. The process worked. In the Korean Conflict 50 percent were willing to shoot and in Vietnam the percent rose to over 90.

- But there was a cost. Many more veterans of Vietnam have suffered from terrible and severe post combat stress than the veterans of other wars.

- The worst news of all, according to Grossman, is that the media everyone watches and uses — movies, shows and news on TV, and reactive video and computer games — use many of the same conditioning processes the army uses to train soldiers to kill in combat. He explains that in real combat training there are safeguards built in, but with the media there are no safeguards. Point and shoot reactive video and computer games are particularly designed to dehumanize the enemy. Grossman believes that one of the main reasons violence has increased in our society is because of these similarities between the effects of combat training and the influence of the media particularly on the young.

A Negative Influence I Choose to Avoid
A Circle Session

Objectives:

— to enable students to share information about negative influences in their lives

— to state publicly that they choose to avoid these influences.

After setting the tone and reviewing the ground rules, introduce the topic in your own words:

Today we are going to focus directly on the kinds of influences we don't need or want in our lives. The topic is 'A Negative Influence I Choose to Avoid.' There are some influences in our lives we know aren't good for us, but can't avoid completely. An example would be having a close relative who deals drugs and keeps trying to get you involved. Those sorts of situations are not our focus for this session. (Although it's a good idea to figure out how to avoid those situations as much as you can.) Instead, we're focusing on influences we can avoid, and choose to avoid, because we under-stand that they are not good for us. Think it

over. If you decide to tell us about a person or group please don't mention their names just tell us what type of influence it is and why you've decided to avoid it. The topic is: 'A Negative Influence I Choose to Avoid.'

After each circle member who wishes to speak has had a chance, conduct a review to reinforce listening skills (if time allows).

Summary Discussion Questions:

— *What is it about these influences that make them unhealthy?*

— *What's the purpose of discussing negative influences in a session like this?*

— *Did anyone mention a negative influence that you hadn't thought of that you will avoid too?*

A Positive Media Influence I Choose for Myself
A Circle Session

Objectives:

— to enable students to acknowledge that their are worthwhile offerings in the media

— to encourage them to become "intentional viewers."

After setting the tone and reviewing the ground rules, introduce the topic in your own words:

Today we are going to discuss the media, but we're not going to criticize it. In fact, our focus is on what's good in the media. The topic is 'A Positive Media Influence I Choose for Myself.' The truth is that there are many very positive media influences — worthwhile, interesting, entertaining, funny and educational movies, documentaries, shows, computer games and learning programs, and types of news programs that inform us, interest us, amuse us, and teach us. What comes to mind for you? It may be hard to just pick one, but try. Pick a program that in some way influences you to

your benefit and tell us about it. The topic is, 'A Positive Media Influence I Choose for Myself.'

After each circle member who wishes to speak has had a chance, conduct a review to reinforce listening skills (if time allows).

Summary Discussion Questions:

— *What were the primary qualities in the programs we mentioned that make them positive influences?*

— *Some people call themselves 'intentional viewers' because they choose to watch programs they see as worthwhile and avoid the others. What do you think of that label?*

— *Did anyone mention a positive media influence that you hadn't thought of that you might look for?*

INFLUENCES OF CHOICE: THE DEVELOPMENTAL ASSETS
Bulletin Board Display Preparation and Discussion
A Culminating Activity

The purpose of this activity is to provide an opportunity for students to consider which individuals, groups, activities, books, movies, etc. are positive influences in their lives. After examining many different types of negative human and media influences in the prior activities in this unit, this culminating activity enables them to generate alternatives — enjoyable, healthy influences they choose as helping them to succeed and grow. An additional, and broader purpose of the activity, is to enlighten students to the realization that they can to some extent *choose* influences they believe will have a positive effect on them and avoid those influences they realize are not conducive to their development and overall well being.

Description:

After listening to a brief presentation of "developmental assets," based on information from the book, "What Kids Need to Succeed,"* the students are invited to bring assorted items for a class bulletin board. Over the period of a week the students create a bulletin board forming a representational collage of influences they recognize as positive in their lives. At the end of the week they are invited to individually tell the class about one or more item(s) they placed on display and why they placed it there. A discussion concludes the activity.

Objectives:

Students will:

— listen to some of the results of a nation-wide survey of over 270,000 young people in 600 communities regarding the positive influences in their lives that allow them to be successful.*

— consider positive influences they choose for themselves and communicate what they are by naming or symbolizing them for a bulletin board display.

— voluntarily describe a positive influence in their lives to the class.

— discuss the importance of examining the myriad influences that surround them with respect to how much each one contributes to their growth and overall happiness.

Time needed:

15 minutes to introduce the activity on the first day; informal time for students to place their items on the bulletin board over the next four days; 20 to 40 minutes for verbal descriptions and discussion on the fifth and final day

Materials needed:

Banner for bulletin board: "Influences of Choice," strips of colored paper and magic markers for slogans and names of influences; optional: art paper and materials

Directions:

1. Introduce this activity by mentioning how the students have been focusing on a lot of influences in their lives and examining them critically. Many of these influences have been seen to have a negative effect. Explain: *Today and for the next four days we are going to start naming positive influences in our lives — people and things we come into contact with that we like, that help us succeed and grow into the people we want to be and are meant to be.*

2. Share the following information with the students:

In their book, 'What Kids Need to Succeed,'* three authors — Peter Benson, Judy Galbraith and Pamela Espeland tell about positive influences in the lives of students. In their book they call these influences "developmental assests." They didn't just decide what those influences are by themselves. They asked the kids — over 270,000 of them in grades six through twelve who live in 600 different communities across the country. The kids told them that they need as many of these helpful influences as possible in their lives in order to be successful:

1. *A family that gives love and support*
2. *Parents kids can turn to for advice and support*
3. *Parents who will take time to talk with, and listen to, their kids*
4. *Other adults, besides parents, who kids can turn to for advice and support*
5. *Other adults who will take time to communicate with kids*
6. *Parents who will help kids succeed in school*
7. *A safe school that encourages and cares about kids*
8. *Parents who are clear about their standards for appropriate behavior*
9. *Parents who set fair and reasonable rules and enforce consequences when the rules are broken*
10. *Parents who know where their kids are, who they are with and how long they will be gone*
11. *Spending at least four nights a week at home*
12. *Friends who are responsible and a good influence*
13. *Involvement in music — band, orchestra, choir or music lessons*
14. *Involvement in extracurricular school activities like sports, clubs and organizations*
15. *Involvement in community activities like clubs and organizations outside of school*
16. *Involvement in a church.*

3. Ask for the students' reactions to the list and then point out: *You might start thinking about what influences in your own life are the most helpful and positive. If you made a list it might have some of the influences I just read and it might have others. Few people have all the positive influences that they could possibly have, but each of us has some.*

4. Explain the activity: *Starting tomorrow you may place items on this bulletin board that are influences you appreciate and choose in your life. We will have the next four days to place our items on it. You could bring a photo of someone or a group. It could be a parent or both parents, a friend*

or friends, an adult who you respect and who is a good example like a relative, a teacher, a counselor, or the pastor or priest of your church, or the rabbi of your synagogue. You may place anything on the bulletin board that shows what the influence is, such as a book or an album cover from a cassette or CD. You might wish to write a short story or create some art to symbolize the positive influence and place it on the bulletin board. (Point out the strips of colored paper and magic markers.) You may also use these strips of paper and magic markers to write a slogan or to name a person, group, place, activity, book, movie, work, church, TV show — whatever or whoever is a positive influence in your life. (Be sure to place some items of your own on the bulletin board too.)

5. On the fifth day, invite the students to individually volunteer to tell the class about one or more items they placed on the bulletin board. Ask them to elaborate on each item and also to explain how it operates in a positive way in their lives. (Be sure to take your turn as well, perhaps going first.)

6. When all of the students who wish to speak about their items have done so, ask the class:

— *What has been the purpose of this activity?*

— *Is it helpful for us to acknowledge the people and things that influence our lives positively?*

— *Can we take control of the ways in which we are influenced?*

— *Have you thought about the fact that you are an influence on others — especially your friends and youngsters who aren't as old as you are? How can you be a positive influence in their lives?*

Guide this discussion to bring out the understanding that by acknowledging and examining the influences in their lives the students empower themselves to take control by avoiding negative influences and seeking positive ones. Encourage them to understand also that they are important influences on others and with that influence comes responsibility.

7. Culminate this activity, and the unit, by sharing this additional information from "What Kids Need to Succeed:"

Remember the positive influences over 270,000 kids told about that the authors listed in their book after they conducted their survey? There were 16 things on that list that are not inside the kids but rather outside, like parents, friends, a safe school, a good church, etc. The authors also found out from the kids that there are some important positive qualities and characteristics kids can have within them and in their own behavior that can help them succeed. They listed 14 of them. Here they are:

1. *Motivation to achieve*
2. *Wanting to graduate from high school and go on with more education after that*
3. *Doing one's best work in school and in other activities*
4. *Completing homework*
5. *Helping other people*
6. *Being concerned about the condition of the world*
7. *Caring about other people — having empathy*
8. *Restraining from sexual activity*
9. *Being assertive*
10. *Being able to make good decisions*
11. *Being able to make and keep friends*

12. *Being able to plan*
13. *Thinking well of oneself — high self esteem*
14. *Having hope.*

8. Point out: *These are assets each of you is responsible for, for yourself. However, the people and conditions in your life influence you strongly. They either help you to develop these behaviors, qualities, and characteristics or they hurt you by discouraging their development within you. That's why it's so important to choose the best influences that you can for your life and avoid the ones that you know aren't good for you to the extent that you are able.*

Language Arts Extension for Adolescents:

Obtain a copy of *What Kids Need to Succeed* and share the information in the section labeled "Tips for Teens: Build Your Own Assets" with your students. Suggest they select one to three tips and work on them and then write about how their efforts turned out after a month has passed.

---

*Peter L. Benson, Ph.D., Judy Galbriath, M.A. and Pamela Espeland, What Kids Need to Succeed: Proven, Practical Ways to Raise Good Kids, Minneapolis, MN: Free Spirit Publishing, Inc. 1995. (612) 338-2068

VIOLENCE CAN BE STOPPED
BEFORE IT STARTS!

OVERVIEW . . .

Sadly, as we all know, violence sometimes occurs unexpectedly due to an individual's hostile, psychotic state. Every means should be made in schools to identify and help singular students with documented tendencies toward such behavior *without mislabeling other students.*

The fact is that violent events caused by students experiencing psychotic breaks are rare. And for that reason this unit is directed at all other students — those "normal" individuals who become stressed, fearful, and angry at times at school and elsewhere. All students become involved in conflicts of various types and all students can profit from learning skills regarding how to manage themselves and resolve those conflicts before physical or psychological violence occurs. As the title suggests, the goal of this unit is to provide kids with as many practical ideas and skills as possible to stop violence before it starts while not compromising their rights and dignity.

Through a variety of active processes, this instructional unit has been designed to provide learning experiences that teach the following information and skills about conflict management:

- Conflicts are normal, inevitable, and occur frequently.

- Conflict occurs within individuals, between individuals, between groups, and between nations.

- Conflict is not necessarily negative but can lead to positive outcomes.

- The worst outcome of a conflict is physical or verbal violence which results in pain and loss of respect for both parties. Another outcome that is almost as bad: pain for one party but respect is diminished for both. The best outcome does not involve physical or verbal attack but rather successful problem solving and enhancement of respect for both parties.

- Blaming is one of the most common causes of conflict escalation. A strategy for avoiding placing blame is to take responsibility for one's own feelings and needs by using "I Messages."

- An assertive mind state and assertive responses to potential conflict situations allow people to stand their ground without taking unfair advantage of others (as in the aggressive style) nor give in to the demands of others to their own detriment (as in the passive style).

- Highly practical conflict management strategies that are almost always effective in numerous everyday situations are: active listening, compromising, postponing, apologizing and/or expressing regret, and problem solving.

- Sometimes life presents seriously sensitive and provocative situations in which serious physical violence could easily erupt. In order to protect themselves and prepare to manage themselves in these situations students can:

  ... reduce their own vulnerability with positive mental statements and images.

  ...consider the consequences before taking action.

  ...defuse a hostile person with calming verbal statements and questions.

  ...respond to bullies with a variety of actions to discourage them.

  ...respond to peer pressure creatively and honestly.

  ...resolve conflicts with mediation strategies.

  ...use proven methods for defusing their own lingering hostility and fear.

Important resources for the development of this unit and excellent sources of additional information and ideas:

- *Aggressive and Violent Students* by Robert P. Bowman, Jo Lynn Johnson, Michael Paget and Mary Thomas-Williams, Chapin, South Carolina: Youth Light, Inc., 1998. Phone: (800) 209-9774.

- *As Tough As Necessary: Countering Violence, Aggression, and Hostility in Our Schools* by Richard L. Curwin and Allen N. Mendler, Alexandria, Virginia: Association for Supervision and Curriculum Development, 1997. Phone: (800) 933-2723.

- *Conflict Resolution Skills for Teens* by David Cowan, M.A., Susanna Palomares, M.S., and Dianne Schilling, M.S., Carson, California: Innerchoice Publishing Company, 1994. Phone: (310) 816-3085.

- *Managing Conflict: Strategies, Activities and Role Plays for Kids* by Susanna Palomares, M.A., and Terri Akin, M.S., Carson, California: Innerchoice Publishing Company, 1995. Phone: (310) 816-3085.

- *Teaching the Skills of Conflict Resolution: Activities and Strategies for Counselors and Teachers* by David Cowan, M.A., Susanna Palomares, M.S., and Dianne Schilling, M.S., Carson, California: Innerchoice Publishing Company, 1992. Phone: (310) 816-3085.

CONFLICT HAPPENS!

Task Groups, Reporting and Class Discussion
An Introductory Activity

Note to teachers and counselors:

This cornerstone activity, and the next one, offer key basic concepts regarding conflict and as such lay the foundation for the ensuing activities that allow students to focus on the skills of managing and resolving conflicts.

The purposes of this activity are to enable students to understand that conflicts: (1) are normal, inevitable, and occur frequently, (3) occur in four major categories: within oneself, between two or more individuals, between groups, and between nations, and (3) are not necessarily negative, but can lead to positive outcomes. The students will also identify and discuss the most negative outcome of a conflict: violence.

Description:

After looking at the labels "Intrapersonal," "Interpersonal," "Intergroup," and "International," and hearing a definition of each one, the students are challenged to generate a brief written description on a chart paper strip of an example for each of the conflict categories and are asked to share their examples with the class. Discussion centers around how common conflict is and how its outcome can be either positive or negative.

Objectives:

Students will:

— learn about the four categories of conflict: intrapersonal, interpersonal, intergroup, and international.

— generate examples of each type of conflict with peers in a task group and then share these examples with the class.

— discuss and consider how conflict can result in positive or negative outcomes.

Time needed:

30 to 50 minutes.

Materials needed:

Four labels with these headings: "Intrapersonal," "Interpersonal," "Intergroup," and "International," and place them side-by-side across the top of a bulletin board or wall, and four strips of chart paper and one magic marker for each task group. (You may wish to provide extras for each group just in case.)

Directions:

1. Introduce this activity with a brief personal story of a conflict you experienced when you were the age of your students. (If this conflict had a positive outcome so much the better, but this is not necessary.)

2. Point out the labels of the four types of conflict, "Intrapersonal," "Interpersonal," Intergroup," and "International," posted side by side at the top of a bulletin board or wall. With a matter-of-fact manner, briefly define each one as the students listen:

- Intrapersonal: conflict within an individual

- Interpersonal: conflict between two or more individuals

- Intergroup: conflict between organizations or groups of people

- International: conflict between nations or countries

3. Ask: *Which category does the conflict I just told you about that I experienced when I was your age, fall into?* Listen to their responses and discuss the four categories just enough to make sure they fully understand each one.

4. Assist the students to form task groups of no more than four members per group. (You may wish to use existing cooperative learning groups, or formulate new ones. If this latter course is taken guide them through a process of determining roles: leader, recorder, process consultant, encourager, etc.)

5. Give the task groups their strips of paper and magic markers. Explain: *Your task will be to come up with an example of a conflict in each category and to write a brief description of it on one of the strips of chart paper. Your leader will ask everyone in your group to focus on the first category and ask for ideas. As soon as everyone who has an idea about that type of conflict has described it, then the leader will ask for a vote on which one your group should select and write down as your example in that category. Then your leader will ask you to focus on the next category. You will have about 10 minutes to hear each others' examples and to discuss them and make choices. After that, each group will report on their examples to the class and we will put them on the bulletin board underneath the labels. Any questions?* As the groups work circulate and listen. Assist only as needed. Let them know when they only have three minutes left.

6. Facilitate the sharing of the groups' examples with the whole class by announcing that each group will give its example of an intrapersonal conflict first. Ask the recorder of each group to stand and show the strip to the class and briefly elaborate on the example. Collect each one. Then focus the attention on the second category: interpersonal conflict. Follow the same procedure for this category and the next two. As the groups' recorders make their presentations maintain your matter-of-fact manner and make as few personal comments as possible. (Adhere the strips to the bulletin board later.)

7. Acknowledge the groups for their fine examples and then assist the students to find the deeper meaning in the activity by conducting a class discussion. Ask:

— *How common is conflict?*

— *Is conflict always bad?*

— *What examples of conflicts did we hear that resulted in positive results for both sides?*

— *What is the worst thing that can result from a conflict?*

Assist the students to acknowledge that conflict is very common — inevitable in fact in everyone's life, but that it is not always a negative occurrence. Sometimes a conflict is just what is needed to clear the air and cause the right and best thing to happen for both parties. Finally, help the students to identify violence as the worst outcome of conflict. Violence has two forms — verbal and physical. Both hurt and complicate matters severely.

8. Explain: *This is the first activity of several that we are going to do in our class which will focus on how to stay out of unnecessary conflicts and get better results from the conflicts that we do get into, instead of allowing them to cause pain to ourselves and others. You already have some of this knowledge and the activities will allow us to share what we know with each other and to learn more. The goal will be to learn a number of skills to manage conflicts and avoid hurtful violence — both verbal and physical.*

Note to Elementary Teachers and Middle and High School Art Teachers: Challenge the students to artistically represent intrapersonal conflict with color and form. A good medium is brightly colored pastels.

Extension for Middle and High School Language Arts:

Encourage students to anonymously write about a memorable conflict they participated in, or observed, with particular focus on their feelings during, immediately after the conflict, and now.

Extension for Social Science — all grades:

As a class examine the sections of the current newspaper, or pull current news stories from the internet, to identify those reporting on conflicts. Challenge the students to categorize the stories into the four categories listed in this activity.

How I Resolved a Conflict Within Myself
A Circle Session

Objectives:

— to allow students to acknowledge the normalcy of experiencing intrapersonal conflicts

— to discuss ways to resolve such conflicts.

After setting the tone and reviewing the ground rules, introduce the topic in your own words:

The topic for this circle session is: 'How I Resolved a Conflict Within Myself.' We have been focusing on types of conflicts people experience including intrapersonal conflict. Have you ever heard that term before? (Listen to responses.) Even if you never heard the term before you have undoubtedly experienced intrapersonal conflicts because everyone does. All of us find that different parts of ourselves are not in agreement from time to time. For example, perhaps part of you likes something and another part of you doesn't. Or maybe at times you have wanted to buy two things but only had money for one and the two sides of

you got into an argument. If you decide to take a turn to speak in this session tell us about your intrapersonal conflict if you would be comfortable doing so and tell us the feelings it gave you. And, of course, tell us how you worked it out with yourself. The topic is: 'How I Resolved a Conflict Within Myself.'

After each circle member who wishes to speak has had a chance, conduct a review to reinforce listening skills (if time allows).

Summary Discussion Questions:

— What were some of the feelings these intrapersonal conflicts caused in us?

— Is intrapersonal conflict normal?

— What were some good ideas you heard for resolving these kinds of conflicts?

WHAT WENT DOWN?
Presentation, Categorizing and Discussion
An Introductory Activity

The purpose of this activity is to assist students to understand that conflicts generally occur in three categories: (1) those involving hostile attack, and possibly violence and result in both parties being hurt and disrespecting each other and themselves; (2) those in which one party attacks (perhaps violently) and "wins" and the other is hurt and "loses" but both disrespect each other and themselves; and (3) neither party attacks in a hostile manner, the matter of contention is settled agreeably, and both parties respect each other and themselves. By recognizing that conflicts can be resolved in the third manner students are becoming prepared to find out how.

Description:

After briefly reviewing the concepts gained in the former activity, the teacher/counselor makes a presentation to the class regarding the three major types of conflict using the handout, "Three Types of Conflict (Or "What Went Down?")." Attention of the class is then focused on some of the conflicts the students described in the former activity. Discussion ensues regarding "what went down?" — which ones were Type 1, Type 2 and Type 3 conflicts. Finally, the class is reminded that the next series of activities will focus on how to manage future conflicts so that they will likely become Type 3 conflicts.

Objectives:

Students will:

— learn about the three types of conflict and find out that it's possible for some conflicts to result in amicable resolution in which no one is hurt and everyone's dignity is preserved (Type 3).

— categorize conflicts into the three types.

— discuss and consider how there are still losses of respect on both sides in Type 2 conflicts.

— discuss and consider how conflict can be managed and positively resolved.

Time needed:

30 to 50 minutes.

Materials needed:

Completed bulletin board (or wall) as described in the prior activity; a copy of the handout, "Three Types of Conflict (Or "What Went Down?")" for each student; a magic marker

Directions:

1. Introduce the activity by pointing out the display on the bulletin board and briefly describe the conflicts students generated in their task groups in the former activity. Review the concepts:

- Conflicts are normal, inevitable and happen frequently in everyone's life.

- They can be intrapersonal, interpersonal, intergroup or international.

- Conflict is not necessarily a bad thing in fact, sometimes the outcome is good for everyone involved.

(This review is particularly important if several days have passed since the former activity occurred.)

2. Explain: *There is another way to categorize conflicts that we are going to take a look at. This way involves three general types of conflict.*

The first type is when both parties become hostile and get out of control. Both are likely to become violent verbally or maybe even physically. When it's over things are generally worse than they were before the conflict and both parties disrespect each other. Both parties also lose self respect even if they won't admit it. This is the most unfortunate type of conflict.

The second type is about as sad. In this type one party is more outwardly hostile and overpowers the other. Verbal and physical violence may occur. The one who overpowers may feel that he, or she, "won" and the one who was overpowered may feel that he, or she, "lost," but there's no respect. Fear, maybe, but both parties disrespect the other and themselves — even the "winner" whether he or she admits it or not.

The third type of conflict is completely different. Things go down in such a way that both parties work it out — they manage and resolve the conflict so that no hostility or verbal or physical violence happens. In fact, in many of these types of conflicts both parties like each other more than they did before. Their respect for each other and themselves is increased!

3. Distribute the handout, to the students and review it with them listening to their comments and answering their questions. If someone asks for more information about how to make Type 3 conflicts happen, respond with, *I'm glad you asked. The next several activities we're doing after this one will give you all of the secrets you desire.*

4. Direct the attention of the class to the bulletin board and challenge the students: *Let's figure out 'what went down' in these conflicts and see how many we can place in the three categories. Were any of them Type 3 conflicts and if so which ones?* Allow individual students to respond and to give their rationale for their categorization. With a magic marker write the numeral 3 beside those the majority of students believe were Type 3 conflicts. To the extent possible, spend most of the time discussing and categorizing Type 3 conflicts. Follow the same procedure for Type 1 and Type 2 Conflicts.

5. Remind the students that in the next series of activities they will learn how to manage future conflicts in such a way that they will likely become Type 3 conflicts.

Extension for Social Science — all grades:

Take the Social Science Extension suggestion in the former activity a step further. After categorizing news stories into the four categories: intrapersonal, interpersonal, intergroup and international, challenge the class to categorize them further into the three types of conflict presented in this activity.

Three Types of Conflict (Or "What Went Down?")

Bodies or feelings get hurt.	One person gets hurt and the other gets his, or her, way.	No one gets hurt.
What happens: Both parties attack each other. Verbal violence (and possibly physical violence) occurs.	**What happens:** One party attacks and overpowers the other using verbal violence (and possibly physical violence).	**What happens:** No one attacks anyone else in a verbal or physical way. Each person speaks for himself, or herself. Each person listens to the other. Both parties agree on a way to settle the conflict.
Results: Things are worse than they were at first. Both parties disrespect each other. Both parties disrespect themselves.	**Results:** The conflict may seem to be settled... BUT Both parties disrespect each other. Both parties disrespect themselves even if the victor won't admit it.	**Results:** The conflict gets settled. Both parties respect each other. Both parties respect themselves.

STOP BLAMING!

Experimentation, Presentation, Writing, Dramatizations and Discussion — A Fundamental Activity

The purposes of this activity are to assist students to understand that blaming is one of the most common causes of conflict escalation, and to provide them with the conflict management skill of expressing disappointment or objection to another person's behavior by taking responsibility for their own feelings about it and expressing what they need and want from the person. The second part of the activity challenges the students to respond in ways that will not escalate conflict when they are the ones who are being justifiably or unjustifiably blamed.

Description:

Part One

A brief review of Type 1, 2 and 3 conflicts is followed by the teacher/counselor addressing the class with "You Messages" and "I Messages," to which students discuss their reactions and chart each response. This is followed by a writing activity in which students write "I Messages" in response to several different hypothetical situations.

Part Two

Scenarios are presented to the class to which students suggest possible responses that would defuse conflict. Next, the students create and write responses aimed at avoiding unnecessary conflict. The activity concludes with a general discussion of "I Messages."

Objectives:

Students will:

— learn the importance of expressing how other peoples' unacceptable actions affect them by using assertive "I Messages" in order to avoid escalating conflicts.

— write and practice using "I Messages."

— learn about and practice apologizing as a response to being blamed for actions they committed.

— learn about and practice responding to being blamed for actions they did not commit by remaining calm and delivering an "I Message."

Time needed:

Two 30 to 50 minute class periods

Materials needed:

Writing materials for students, whiteboard, chalkboard or chart with magic markers

Directions:

Part One: Formulating "I Messages"

1. Introduce the activity's purpose by briefly reviewing the differences between Type 1, 2 and 3 conflicts as examined in the prior activity. Explain: *Have you ever noticed that some people have lots*

of friends and rarely get into fights with anyone? This isn't because they never have things happen that could lead to a fight. Sometimes they do find themselves in a conflict and when that happens they usually have a way of settling things easily and quickly with the other person so that they remain friends. Their conflicts are usually Type 3 conflicts. These people aren't magic — they just have a power they know they have, and they know how to use it! You have the same power. This activity will show it to you. It will also get you started using it so you can stay out of unnecessary painful conflicts and turn many of the conflicts you have into Type 3 conflicts.

2. Initiate the activity by suggesting: *Let's try something. Imagine that I am talking with you privately about not turning in your homework. Listen to my message about it and then notice how it makes you feel.*

3. Deliver a "You Message." It could go something like this:

You failed to turn in your homework again — probably because you didn't do it, and even if you did, you're so forgetful and disorganized that you left it at home. You better watch it. You're not going to get a passing grade if you continue to be so flaky.

4. Ask: *How did that make you feel?* Listen to, and chart, the students' responses. If no one mentions "blaming" or "accusing," ask them if they felt "blamed," or "accused." You will undoubtedly hear "yes." Add these words to the list on the chart.

5. Without further discussion tell the students that there will now be a replay of the very same situation, but with a variation in your words and tone. Ask the students to notice how this message makes them feel. Then deliver an "I Message." It could go something like this:

I'm concerned and disappointed that you didn't turn in your homework. I'm concerned because doing the homework for this class is necessary for you to learn all the information and skills you need in order to get the grade you are capable of getting. I want to see that homework next time, okay?

6. Ask:

— *How did that make you feel?*

— *Did I blame you the second time or just explain how I felt about your not turning in your homework and why it concerned me?*

— *Which time did I seem to care about you?*

— *Which time did you feel more like making a remark to get even with me?*

7. Help the students pinpoint their understanding of the differences between the two messages and their effect on people. Chart their responses to the "I Message" and explain:

The first message was a 'You Message.' I blamed and accused you several times by saying, 'you' this and 'you' that. I started each sentence with the word, 'you.' People who have the power to avoid unnecessary conflicts, and to easily and quickly settle conflicts they are in, never or rarely delivered 'You Messages' because they know that it will make the other person feel angry, hurt, and up for a fight. They know that even if the person they deliver a 'You Message' to doesn't say anything back at that moment they are likely to get even later in some way.

The second message was an 'I Message.' I told you how I felt about your not turning in your homework and I told you why. Both sentences were started with the word, 'I.' Here's the formula: (Write this on the chalkboard.)

1. *I feel*

2. *when you*

3. *because...*

4. *what I need/want from you is...*

It takes some courage to use an 'I Message' because when you do it you are talking about yourself — your feelings and your wishes. You aren't dumping blame on someone else. Using an 'I message' is a smart way to talk to people when you are mad at them or frustrated by something they have done. With an 'I Message' you express your own concerns. In order to express them, you have to be honest with yourself and recognize what your concerns are. When the listener hears your 'I Message' the listener knows that he or she has done something you object to and feel bad about. By delivering an 'I Message' you can make a strong, assertive statement without making the listener feel blamed which no one likes even when guilty. This is a clear way to tell people how you feel and what you want and need from them without causing them to want to get even. It's a great conflict management secret.

8. Begin the writing exercise by asking the students to use the four point formula (above) to write an "I Message" to situations you will now present verbally. (The students may work together in pairs or individually.) Here are some hypothetical situations:

You come home from school and find your younger brother or sister, cousin, or neighbor child looking into your dresser drawer and handling your personal things. You are understandably displeased. You stop yourself from delivering a 'You Message.' Instead you deliver an 'I Message.'

You loan one of your favorite cassettes, or a CD, to one of your friends who hasn't returned it for a long time. When you ask about it your friend admits that it's been lost. You're angry and feel like delivering a 'You Message,' but instead you deliver an 'I Message.'

All of your friends' parents are letting them go to a concert you want to attend too. But your parent, or parents, say no. You feel like delivering a 'You Message,' but instead you deliver an 'I Message.'

9. After the students have written their responses to each of the hypothetical situations, ask for their attention. Focus on one situation at a time encouraging volunteers to read their 'I Messages' aloud. Some of the responses may also be acted out. After each one is read, and possibly dramatized, discuss how it allows them to stand up for themselves and defuse the situation at the same time. Allow some discussion and laughter about the 'You Messages,' the students probably felt like delivering and what the unpleasant consequences of those messages might have been.

Part Two: Responding to "You Messages"

10. Begin by posing this question to the students: *No one is perfect and sometimes it is you who has done something that is objectionable to another person. If the person delivers an 'I Message,' it's not likely that a heated conflict will result because the 'I Message' is respectful and not accusatory. But how would you handle yourself if the person blames and accuses you with a 'You Message'?*

11. Present the following scenario and ask the students to suggest possible responses that would defuse conflict.

As you are walking to class with your friend, he shows you some photos he took of you and some of your other friends. You ask to hold them yourself so you can see them better but then you spot the water fountain. You are thirsty so you stop for a quick drink. Things get awkward and the photos slip. All of them get wet and start to stick to each other. Your friend sees what's happening and raising his voice says, 'You klutz! You're a walking disaster. Look what you did. You ruined them!' This bothers you, but you don't want a fight. How do you respond?

12. Listen to the students' suggestions and assist them to acknowledge that a sincere apology and an offer to correct the damage to the extent possible is appropriate along with a calm statement that calling you names and yelling is not necessary. Excusing and explaining what happened and how it happened usually only inflames the other person and the inevitable result is heated conflict. Invite one or more pairs of students to dramatize the scene with an emphasis on how to defuse the situation while retaining dignity.

13. Change focus. Point out: *Sometimes someone delivers a 'You Message' and you did not do what they are blaming you for. It's harder then not to become righteously indignant and create a heated conflict with your response. This is the most challenging situation for defusing conflict.* Present the following scenario and ask the students to suggest possible responses that would defuse conflict.

Let's imagine that your friend starts to deliver a 'You Message' about your not returning a jacket, but that you actually did return it. Your friend says, 'you can't be trusted; you are irresponsible; you never return things, etc.' But, in fact, your friend doesn't remember that you returned it and then she lost it. You are annoyed, but you don't want a yelling and screaming contest. What do you say without backing down and how do you say it?

14. Listen to the students' suggestions for this situation. Help them recognize that the best response to a 'You Message' of this kind is a calmly delivered 'I Message' if they wish to use their power to avoid unnecessary conflict. Invite one or more pairs of students to dramatize the scene with an emphasis on how to resolve the problem peacefully.

15. Invite the students to generate situations in which they are being blamed justifiably and unjustifiably. Challenge them to write responses aimed at avoiding unnecessary conflict or evenhandedly resolving conflict that has begun. Ask for volunteers to read, and perhaps act out, their responses.

16. Conclude with a general discussion. Invite the students to respond to the following questions:

— *What are the main reasons for delivering 'I Messages' instead of 'You Messages?'*

— *There are times when it isn't easy to deliver an 'I Message.' Why is that?*

— *In what way does it take courage to deliver an 'I Message?'*

A Conflict I Observed
A Circle Session

Objectives:

— to allow students to acknowledge the frequency of conflicts

— to identify the actions participants can take to escalate those conflicts or manage and resolve them.

After setting the tone and reviewing the ground rules, introduce the topic in your own words:

Today our topic is, 'A Conflict I Observed.' Everyone has observed other people in some sort of conflict — a full blown fight about who's to blame for something, an argument between friends about how to spend some time together, or a squabble between two kids about whose turn it is to do a chore. If you decide to take a turn in this session you may tell about a well managed conflict which had a good outcome for everyone or one where lots of blaming occurred and the outcome was not good for anyone. Also, tell us how the conflict made you feel as an observer without telling us who

was involved or your relationship to them. Our topic is: 'A Conflict I Observed.'

After each circle member who wishes to speak has had a chance, conduct a review to reinforce listening skills (if time allows).

Summary Discussion Questions:

— *How many of the conflicts that we discussed were well managed and turned out well for everyone?*

— *What caused the conflicts with bad outcomes to turn out that way?*

— *What about respect? Which people were respectful of each other? Which ones seemed to respect themselves? Which ones did you respect and disrespect and why?*

A Time I Used an 'I Message' with a Successful Result

A Circle Session

Objective:

— to enable students to examine how the nonblaming, assertive strategy of using "I Messages" is effective in managing and resolving conflicts.

After setting the tone and reviewing the ground rules, introduce the topic in your own words:

In our class we have been focusing recently on how important it is to stop blaming in conflict situations and to take responsibility for your own feelings and for what you want by using 'I Messages.' By now you may have had a chance to try this. In fact, our topic is: 'A Time I Used an 'I Message' with a Successful Result.' Have you tried this yet? If so, we would like to hear about the situation and what your 'I Message' was. If you take a turn tell us how the other person or people responded

without telling us who it was or your relationship to them. Our topic is: 'A Time I Used an 'I Message' with a Successful Result.'

After each circle member who wishes to speak has had a chance, conduct a review to reinforce listening skills (if time allows).

Summary Discussion Questions:

— What were some of the 'I Messages' that were used?

— What were the results of using 'I Messages' in the situations we heard about?

— Did you get any new ideas for ways to use 'I Messages' from this session?

BE ASSERTIVE!

Presentation, Dyads, Dramatization and Discussion
A Fundamental Activity

The purposes of this activity are to provide students with an understanding of the mind states and behaviors that characterize an effective model for conflict management (the assertive style) and to contrast it to those of two ineffective models (the aggressive and the passive styles). The activity also allows students the opportunity to practice using the assertive style.

Description:

The meaning of the words "Aggressive," "Assertive," and "Passive" are discussed. The students then complete and discuss the handout, "The Art of Being Assertive." Next, as pairs of students create, dramatize and discuss demonstrations of assertive behavior. A general discussion concludes the activity.

Objectives:

Students will:

— understand the difference between the mind states and behavior of aggressive, assertive, and passive styles of responding to situations.

— discriminate between responses of each type.

— work with a partner to generate, plan and render a dramatization of an assertive response to a situation.

— consider and discuss the merits of assertive thinking and actions as opposed to aggressive and passive mind states and actions.

Time needed:

One 30 to 50 minute class period. A second partial or full class period may be needed for completing the dramatizations.

Materials needed:

One copy of the handout, "The Art of Being Assertive" for each student; chalkboard

Directions:

1. Introduce the activity. As the students observe, write the terms: "Aggressive," "Assertive," and "Passive" on the chalkboard. Explain: *Today we are going to continue to learn the secrets of people who know how to avoid unnecessary conflicts and easily resolve the ones they do get into. These people have a style of responding to potential conflict situations and it's one of these three styles. Let me tell you about them:* (You may wish to provide examples of well known characters in literature or the media to augment these descriptions.)

Aggressive people are often thought of as pushy, hotheads, or bullies. They frequently take advantage of other people when they get a chance. They usually don't play fair. They frequently overpower other people with hostility and harsh words as well as other forms of verbal violence like strong 'You Messages.' Sometimes they even become physically violent.

Assertive people don't resort to the tactics of aggressive people, but they are not wimps! They stand up for themselves while remaining cool and calm. They are respectful but direct about their feelings, needs, and desires. They use "I Messages," instead of "You Messages." They are confident and they know their rights. However they know and respect the rights of others as well.

Passive people are the wimps. They are often afraid to stand up for themselves and they frequently let other people take advantage of them. They put themselves down, apologize when they should be the one apologized to, and constantly seek the approval of others.

2. Determine through discussion of the three types that the style in the middle, the "Assertive Style" is the one used by people who know how to successfully avoid and resolve conflicts.

3. Distribute the handout, "The Art of Being Assertive" and review the first part with the class which provides descriptions of assertive, aggressive and passive mind states and behaviors. Be sure to emphasize that assertive actions emanate from an assertive mind state in which the person talks to him/herself in positive and honest ways about what he/she feels and needs. The assertive person knows his/her rights and knows that other people have rights too. This person controls his/her anger, nervousness, anxiety, or fear instead of letting these feelings control him/her.

4. Direct the class to form dyads for discussing and completing the exercise in the second part of the handout in which they label examples of the three types of mind states and behaviors. After the students have completed the exercise, review their responses as a class.

5. Present this challenge to the dyads: *Work with your partner to come up with a situation you could act out for the class in which a person has the choice to react aggressively, assertively or passively. Both of you should take a role in the dramatization. Your task is for one of you to demonstrate an assertive response.*

6. Give the students a time limit for planning and rehearsal. Be available to them if they need clarification or suggestions.

7. Invite the pairs of students to present their dramatizations. (You may need a second class session to complete these.) Ask each pair of students to explain the setting and situation to the class before they begin to dramatize it. Lead the class in applause at the end of each performance and briefly discuss each dramatization using some or all of the following questions:

— *What were the assertive statements in this dramatization?*

— *How well did the assertive approach seem to work to settle the matter while not giving in to the other person?*

— *What other assertive types of responses might have been made?*

— *What might have an aggressive response been?*

— *If an aggressive response was made what probably would have happened next?*

— What might have a passive response been?

— If a passive response was made what probably would have happened next?

8. After all of the dramatizations have been enacted and discussed, conclude with a culminating discussion using the following questions:

— The kinds of situations we have been focusing on would cause anyone to feel anger, nervousness, anxiety, or even fear. Who is best able to keep these feelings from controlling them but instead controls the feelings — the aggressive person, the assertive person, or the passive person?

— In what ways does it take courage and self control to act assertively?

— If you find that you are facing a touchy situation and you want to respond assertively first you need to get a hold of yourself. Then, what kinds of thoughts do you need to think to create the best mind state before you act?

THE ART OF BEING ASSERTIVE

What is the mind state of the assertive person? His or her thoughts are:

- "I know that all people are equally important including myself."
- "I know how I feel, what I need, and what I want. I can state my feelings, needs and wants to other people when I choose to."
- "I have the right to ask for what I want or need and other people have the right to say yes or no. I can't complain if I don't get what I wanted but didn't ask for it."
- "Other people have an equal right to ask for what they want or need. And I have the right to say yes or no."
- "If I don't understand a situation I can ask questions to find out what I need to know."

How does the assertive person act?

- Assertive people express themselves openly and honestly to communicate their feelings, wants and needs without demanding them.
- They also show respect for the feelings, wants and needs of others.
- When they don't understand what's going on they ask questions.

What is the mind state of the aggressive person? His or her thoughts are:

- "Get them before they get you."
- "The best defense is an offense."
- "How you play doesn't count, only that you win."
- "Never give a sucker an even break."
- "Don't bother to think things over or get into discussions; just do what you have to do."

How does the aggressive person act?

- Aggressive people intentionally attack, take advantage of, humiliate, hurt or put other people down.
- They are usually outraged if anyone treats them the same way.
- Jump to conclusions and react to situations based on assumptions that are often not correct.

What is the mind state of the passive person? His or her thoughts are:

- "Other people are more important than me."
- "I should never cause anyone to be disappointed or disapprove of me."
- "I should never say no to anyone for any reason."
- "I should never give anyone a stomach ache or headache except myself."
- "I don't have the right to ask questions about situations I don't understand."

How does the passive person act?

- Passive people permit or invite others to take advantage of them or hurt or humiliate them.
- They frequently put themselves down.
- They rarely speak up with their opinion or to ask questions about situations they don't understand.

TRY THIS . . .

For each of the following situations write in the words "Assertive," "Aggressive," and "Passive," next to the description of a mind state or a behavior of each type:

Before class Mark approaches Ahmet and says: "Quick. Let me see your homework." Ahmet asks why and Mark says, "So I can copy it. Quit stalling."

Ahmet's thoughts before he does anything are:

_____ "I did the work and he didn't. It's not fair for him to take advantage of me like this. I'm going to tell him so."

_____ "I better give it to him because he'll get mad and start calling me names if I don't."

_____ "What nerve! I'm going to tell him what an insufferable jerk he is."

■ ■

Marlene is a high school freshman. One morning her parents asked her to babysit James, her younger brother, after school that afternoon. Marlene agreed and came home as soon as school was over and waited for James to come home too. (He attended the afternoon kindergarten class.) She waited and waited but there was no sign of James who went to a friend's house and forgot all about coming home. Marlene was becoming so worried about James she was frantic. She called the homes of several of his friends but no one she talked to knew where he was. Finally, two hours late, James walked in through the front door. The minute Marlene saw him she said:

_____ "You miserable, inconsiderate little brat! Where on earth have you been? I'm gonna teach you a lesson you'll never forget!"

_____ "James, boy! Thank goodness you're here. I didn't know what to do. Please don't tell Mom and Dad that I couldn't find you and get you to come home."

_____ "James, I've been waiting two hours for you to come home. I've been extremely worried about you and I'm very angry at you. I want to know where you've been and what you've been doing?"

■■■

Angela's family has recently moved into the neighborhood so she's "the new girl." She wants to make friends so whenever she can she smiles at the other students and says "Hi." When she greets Randy he stops to talk with her in a friendly way. Later Randy's girlfriend, Tess, approaches Angela. Tess says:

_____ "Hi, Angela. I'm Tess. I've noticed how friendly you are. In fact, I saw you talking with my boyfriend a few minutes ago. His name is Randy. Would you like to sit with us at lunch?"

_____ "Gee, you're cute, Angela. Randy will probably want you to be his girlfriend instead of me."

_____ "Hey you, whatever your name is! Just keep your grubby hands off Randy. He's mine!"

■■■

Mr. Harris teaches five science classes and one math class. Each class has about thirty-five students which means he has over 200 students' names to learn at the beginning of each semester. One day during the first week of class he calls a student "Bob," whose name is actually Rob. Rob reacts in an insulting manner saying, "Can't anyone get my name right? It's Rob, old man." Before responding Mr. Harris thinks to himself:

_____ "What a twerp! I'll find a way to put him in his place soon enough."

_____ "What's wrong with me? I did it again. I wish I could remember names better."

_____ "I don't like his attitude but I understand his feelings. That probably happens to him a lot."

A Time I Stood My Ground
A Circle Session

Objectives:

— to enable students to take credit for assertive behavior

— to examine how the behavior emanated from an assertive mind state.

After setting the tone and reviewing the ground rules, introduce the topic in your own words:

Recently in our class we have been learning about three mind states and ways of taking action that come from each one. They are often referred to as 'styles' — the aggressive, assertive, and passive styles. We've learned that the one in the middle, the assertive style, usually works best for managing conflicts so that everyone can come out okay. Our topic today is, 'A Time I Stood My Ground.' Think about a situation you faced where you were bothered in some way and when you talked with the person or people who were involved you weren't aggressive and you weren't passive, letting them run over you, either. If you acted in an assertive way you stated your feelings and asked for what you needed and wanted and

you probably succeeded to some extent. If you decide to take a turn tell us about it — what your thoughts were, what you said, and what you did that was assertive. Tell us the results too. Just don't say the names of the other people involved. Our topic is: 'A Time I Stood My Ground.'

After each circle member who wishes to speak has had a chance, conduct a review to reinforce listening skills (if time allows).

Summary Discussion Questions:

— What were some assertive statements we heard about that really worked well?

— How does it help us to get into an assertive mind state before talking with the person or people in the situation?

— Did you get any new ideas for ways to be assertive from this session?

WORK IT OUT!

Presentation, Task Groups, Dramatization and Discussion
A Fundamental Activity

The purposes of this activity are to provide students with an assortment of strategies for managing and resolving conflicts including active listening, compromising, postponing, apologizing and/or expressing regret, and problem solving, and to allow them to dramatize and discuss each one.

Description:

The students are presented with five strategies for managing and resolving conflict both through discussion and a handout. Task groups are formed and each group creates a situation and plans a dramatization featuring one of the five strategies. A general discussion concludes the activity.

Objectives:

Students will:

— learn about, practice, and discriminate between, five strategies for managing and resolving conflict.

— work with several classmates in a task group to generate, plan and render a dramatization in which they will demonstrate one of the strategies.

— observe dramatizations of other task groups and guess which strategy was demonstrated.

— Discuss the possibilities and advantages of using all five strategies in future life situations.

Time needed:

One 30 to 50 minute class period. A second partial class period may be needed for completing the dramatizations.

Materials needed:

One copy of the handout, "Five Strategies for Managing and Resolving Conflict" for each student; chalkboard

Directions:

1. Introduce the activity. As the students observe, write the terms: "Active Listening," "Compromising," "Postponing," "Apologizing and/or Expressing Regret," and "Problem Solving" on the chalkboard. Explain: *Lately in this class we have been concerned with how to avoid unnecessary conflicts and how to manage and resolve conflicts we do get into. We have learned about Type 3 conflicts in which no one gets hurt, how to use 'I Messages,' and how to be assertive. But there are still other strategies that all of us have the power to use any time we choose. Let's take a look at each one of them.*

2. Distribute the handout, "Five Strategies for Managing and Resolving Conflict" and review it carefully with the students including the exercises at the end. As you read about each strategy together provide a brief example of a conflict you have experienced, or observed, and tell how the strategy was used, or could have been used, to resolve it. The students may also be invited to provide examples. This makes the information more interesting and assures greater understanding.

3. Assist the students to form five task groups — one for each strategy. An alternative: Form 10 groups, two per strategy. The ideal group size is four students.

4. Without the other groups hearing, give each task group a strategy to enact for the class in a dramatization. Explain: *Each group has one of the strategies. Your group's task is to decide among you on a conflict situation that this strategy might help to resolve. You will plan a dramatization of the situation. If possible all members of your group should participate in some way in the dramatization. Plan it so that at least one of you will demonstrate the use of your group's conflict management strategy. Then the class will guess which one you are demonstrating.* Give the students a time limit for planning and rehearsal. Be available to them if they need help.

5. Call on the groups to render their dramatizations in a random order. After each one ask the class to guess which strategy was demonstrated. Then lead an applause and a brief discussion. Ask:

— *How did you know which strategy was being demonstrated?*

— *How well did it work?*

— *Were there other ways the strategy could have been used?*

— *Were there other strategies that could have been used, including the use of an 'I Message,' or making an assertive statement?*

6. After all of the dramatizations and discussions, conclude the activity with a culminating discussion. Ask the students:

— *Why have we been learning about ways to manage and resolve conflict? Does it really do any good?"*

— *In order to use any of the strategies we have learned, what do you have to do first, within yourself, when you find yourself in a conflict situation?"*

— *If you completely forget to use a conflict management strategy and find yourself in a heated fight is it too late? Is there anything you can do as soon as you realize what's happened?"*

Turn Students to Their Computers:

The Coolien Challenge and Central High, Two interactive CD Roms address problem solving in potential conflict situations and related topics. They are especially beneficial for those who enjoy learning at the computer. Available from: Compu-Teach in Redmond, Washington (800) 448-3224.

FIVE STRATEGIES FOR MANAGING AND RESOLVING CONFLICT

Active Listening:

Have you ever noticed how you feel when you are upset about something and the other person, or people, involved won't listen? It just makes things worse. The opposite is also true: one of the best ways to settle a tense situation with someone is to listen. Just stop talking and start listening. To do it right you have to be respectful and sincere and silent no matter how much you want to say something. When you use this strategy you lean forward, look into the person's eyes, and really try to understand him or her especially his or her feelings and opinions. Just keep listening and finally he or she will be ready to listen to you. But it will be awhile so be very, very patient. This strategy works like a charm!

Compromising:

Let's say an impossible situation has presented itself: you and another person both want the same thing at the same time. So you suggest a compromise that allows each of you to get some of it. You could share something like a candy bar, or take turns using something like a pair of roller blades. The way you use this strategy is to offer to give up something if the other person will do the same. The key is that you make the offer and you show that you will give up your part first. This almost always causes the other person to want to cooperate. (If the thing you both want can't be divided or if the other person refuses to compromise, suggest flipping a coin.)

Postponing:

Have you ever noticed how fights usually happen when one or both people are in a bad mood, hungry, or tired? The strategy of postponing is exactly that — you suggest that you put off discussing the matter and get back to it later. You could say, "Look, Sam, I've had a long day and I feel lousy. Could we get back to this tomorrow?" or "I've got an idea. Let's go eat and talk about this afterward. I'm so starved I can't think straight. What about you?" Do be sure to get back with the person later at the agreed-upon time and then start out with active listening.

Apologizing and/or Expressing Regret:

Sometimes a sincere apology and admitting your mistake is the best strategy when you have actually offended someone and they have become upset as anyone would. But there are times when you didn't do exactly what they think you did. Accidents are a good example. You may have caused an accident somehow, but you never intended anyone to get hurt. That's when you might prefer to express regret. You might say, "It's terrible that that happened. I don't blame you for feeling mad." or "I'm sorry it happened. I didn't do it on purpose. Here, let me help." When the other person knows you feel regret and you care about him or her it makes a huge difference.

Problem Solving:

Sometimes things can get complicated between you and another person. With the strategy of problem solving you use as many of the other strategies as you can especially active listening, I messages, and a calm, respectful voice. If you don't understand the other person, don't interrupt. When he or she finishes talking explain that you don't understand and ask "What exactly do you mean?" and listen some more. Then see if you can define the problem without any blaming. Take the attitude that the two of you are against the problem, not against each other. Brainstorm ideas for solutions to the problem together and then agree on one or more that seem to make the most sense. If you can't agree on a solution, postpone deciding until later after each of you has had a chance to think about it some more.

Situations and Strategies:

Dan and Stan are 16 year-old twins. Both are learning to drive. They are in a conflict about who will get to drive with their Dad for an hour before dinner. They have both finished their homework. Their Dad is home but has to go out to a meeting after dinner. Dinner is in one hour.

If you were Dan or Stan what strategy (or strategies) would you use to manage this conflict?

Han and Sharifah are partners in a social science research project. They have been told that they may pick their own topic but they can't agree on one they both like. All the other teams have begun work but Han and Sharifah are stuck. Both of them are becoming more annoyed with each other as the due date for their report gets closer and closer.

If you were Han or Sharifah what strategy (or strategies) would you use to manage this conflict?

Julia comes home from school to find her Mom very upset about something that all the kids in the family have done, including Julia. She tries to figure out what they did but it isn't clear. Her Mom just keeps going on and on about how "all you kids just keep messing everything up." Julia is starting to feel frustrated and impatient.

If you were Julia what strategy (or strategies) would you use to manage this conflict?

Vinnie and Alex are in the cafeteria heading for a table after filling their trays with food. Vinnie is following Alex and accidentally trips. This upsets Vinnie because he will have to go back for more food. But it upsets Alex more because his back got splashed with some very red spaghetti sauce. Alex starts to yell at Vinnie calling him a klutz.

If you were Vinnie, what strategy (or strategies) would you use to manage this conflict?

Mr. Tyler and Mr. Garcia are both teachers in a middle school and they both teach six classes. They are on a committee to plan a carnival at the school. One day neither of them get to eat lunch because of problems they had to handle during lunch period. They had agreed a few days ago to meet with each other that afternoon after school to discuss plans for the carnival. Unfortunately both men are tired and hungry. As they talk they discover that neither one likes any of the suggestions the other one makes. They can't seem to agree on anything and both of them are becoming irritable.

If you were Mr. Tyler or Mr. Garcia what strategy (or strategies) would you use to manage this conflict?

I Accidentally Made Someone Mad
A Circle Session

Objectives:

— to allow students to acknowledge that at times they are the ones who offend others

— to discuss how to respond if the people they offend react with blaming.

After setting the tone and reviewing the ground rules, introduce the topic in your own words:

Our topic for this session is 'I Accidentally Made Someone Mad.' We have been learning all about how to handle ourselves when someone has made us mad, but there are times in everyone's life when it works the other way. You can control yourself and use conflict management strategies when someone has done something you object to. But think about a time when the shoe was on the other foot and without meaning to you upset someone and he or she reacted with blaming. What did you do and how did it work? Did you try to understand the person, listen, use an 'I Message,' apologize, express regret or use any of the other strategies we've been learning about? Or did you become aggressive or passive? If you'd like to take a turn, tell us about an incident like this and how you feel about it now, but don't tell us who the other person was. The topic is: 'I Accidentally Made Someone Mad.'

After each circle member who wishes to speak has had a chance, conduct a review to reinforce listening skills (if time allows).

Summary Discussion Questions:

— What happened in most of the situations where both people became aggressive?

— What happened in most of the situations where a conflict management strategy like active listening, apologizing or expressing regret was used?

— Did you get any ideas for ways to respond when someone blames you for something even if you didn't do it on purpose?

WHEN THE GOING GETS TOUGH

Task Groups, Student (or Teacher/Counselor) Presentations and Class Discussion — A Fundamental Activity

The purpose of this activity is to enable the students to teach each other how to prepare mentally, emotionally and behaviorally to seriously provoking situations in order to avoid or stop violence. These include: (1) reducing one's own psychological vulnerability, (2) considering consequences, (3) verbal defusing of extreme hostility, (4) verbal response to bullying and ridicule, (5) verbal resistance to peer pressure, (6) resolving conflicts with mediation, and (7) using methods for defusing one's own hostility and fear.

Description:

Part One

After a brief review of key concepts presented in the unit's prior activities, the students are divided into seven task groups, each having its own presentation topic and information to "teach" to the class. The balance of the class period is devoted to preparing the presentations in a creative way.

Part Two

Each task group makes its presentation to the class followed by a brief teacher/counselor-led discussion. After all the presentations have been made the teacher/counselor leads a culminating discussion regarding the overall implications of the information provided by the students.

Objectives:

Students will:

— discuss a concept related to seriously provocative situations with several other students in a task group and plan with them how to present the information to the class in a subsequent class session.

— observe, listen to, and consider concepts presented by students in other task groups.

— participate in class discussions that relate to each presentation and to a culminating discussion regarding acknowledgment of their own abilities to mentally, emotionally and behaviorally respond to provocative situations in order to avoid or stop violence.

Time needed:

Two class sessions: one for planning and one (perhaps two) for presentations and discussion.

Materials needed:

The seven "Ideas to Consider" sheets for the task groups and materials for visual aids that some of the task groups might need.

Directions:

Part One: Presentation Planning

1. Introduce the activity by sharing a personal anecdote in which you recently and successfully used one of the conflict management strategies presented in one of the prior activities in this unit. Invite the students to do likewise.

2. Explain: *We have learned a lot about how to deal with conflict. We know it's normal and inevitable in our lives. We know that some conflicts are helpful and make things better if they are managed well. However, everyone knows that more serious situations than the ones we have focused on could arise here at school and in other places. Sometimes the going can really get tough. There are times when someone becomes extremely hostile and potentially violent. Sometimes you might feel frightened just to be at school because you fear that violence could occur. Sometimes someone might bully you, or embarrass you in front of other people, or bait you to fight. Sometimes some other students might put pressure on you to do something destructive or illegal and you really don't want to do it. Sometimes you could possibly get upset and angry yourself and feel like doing some damage. These are extremely sensitive situations and in this activity we are going to take a look at all of them and learn about possible ways to handle them.*

3. Assist the students to form seven task groups. (Ideal size would be no more than four members per group.) An alternative: Form 14 groups, two per presentation topic.

4. Explain the task: *In this activity you are going to be the 'teachers.' Your group will be given a topic about a serious conflict issue. Then you will plan how to 'team teach' the information and ideas to the rest of us in a three to ten minute lesson. You will have the rest of the class period for planning. (In the next class period(s) the groups will make their presentations.)*

5. Distribute the seven "Ideas to Consider" sheets, one per group. Suggest: *Read the information and discuss it among yourselves. Then plan an interesting way to teach it to us. Be creative. You could use examples. If your group plans to demonstrate a strategy with a dramatization or have the class practice using a strategy, that will be useful. You might have a short story to tell that would help to make one or two of your points. I'm available to help if you need me.* Circulate as the groups discuss the information and begin planning their presentations serving as a consultant as needed.

Part Two: Presentations and Discussion

6. Call on each task group to make its presentation in the order given below. Model attentive listening skills and lead an applause at the end of each presentation. After each one, lead a short discussion by asking the class:

— *What were some of the most useful ideas the group presented?*

— *Can you suggest some additional ideas for handling this type of issue or situation?*

— *What questions do you have for the presenters?*

The titles of the seven presentations* are:

    I. Arm Yourself Mentally

    II. Consider the Consequences

    III. Defuse Hostility**

    IV. Refuse the Bait**

    V. Handle the Pressure**

    VI. Resolve Problems with Mediation

    VII. Chill Yourself Out

7. Culminate with a summary discussion. Ask the class:

— *In all the presentations what ideas were the most interesting and helpful for you?*

— *In many of the presentations we heard ideas for what we could do. We also heard ideas for ways to think. How does it help to learn ways to think when you are in a tough situation?*

— *You can't control what other people think and do, but you can control what you think and do. Could that make some difference when the going gets tough?*

Listen to all of the comments students make and make your own in response to the questions as well. Guide the discussion to help the students acknowledge their own power to alter provocative situations through self control, clear thinking, and skillful action.

Extension Activity for all grade levels:

Facilitate the creation of dramatic scenarios with the students of situations involving hostile people, bullies, and peer pressure to allow them opportunities to practice using the strategies suggested in "Ideas to Consider" sheets numbers III, IV and V.

Arm Yourself Mentally

Ideas to Consider #1

Have you ever noticed how some people seem strong and rarely get picked on while others seem to be the victim more often than anyone else? The ones who seem strong might not even be very big or physically strong, but it's as if they are protected in some way. Frequent victims might be big and physically strong, but it almost seems like they are wearing a sign that says, "Hit me."

Are some people really protected while others are not? Yes! But their protection is not weapons or shields. Nor is it magic. It's just the way they think and feel about themselves. They are confident and they are in control of themselves and they know it. They trust in their own ability to handle situations, even tough ones. Their confident thoughts and feelings show in their manner and actions — what they say and do — even the way they walk! Bullies rarely pick these people to mess with because it's so much easier to torment the ones who are not confident in themselves and show weakness and fear.

The protection of inner strength and confidence is available to everyone. You can have it too. If you don't feel confident inside you can teach it to yourself. Just like physical exercise to make your body strong, you can do mental exercises to make your personality strong. In fact, most famous athletes do both!

For mental training think positive thoughts about yourself and imagine yourself with a shield around you that mean words bounce off of. Never, ever put yourself down out loud or in your thoughts. If you catch yourself doing it, turn the thought around. If you say "I'm so dumb," to yourself, say "I'm so smart," to correct it. In fact, say "I'm smart," to yourself many times each day.

Besides, "I'm smart," here are some other positive thoughts you can train yourself to think and believe about yourself. Say them many times to yourself each day:

> *"I can handle problems."*
> *"When the going gets tough, I can figure out what to do."*
> *"I can calm down and breathe when I feel upset."*
> *"I trust myself."*
> *"I care about people and they care about me."*

One word of caution: don't overdo it and come off arrogant. That invites people to want to bring you down.

Consider the Consequences

Ideas to Consider #2

When people in prison are asked, "What do you want to say to kids?" their answer is almost always the same: "Think about the consequences of what you are about to do before you do it. Don't (pick a fight, take a bully's bait, shoot, drive drunk, take drugs, steal, take advantage of someone, threaten, talk bad about someone behind his or her back, or put somebody down) until you stop and think about what could happen if you do it."

This is their answer because they have had many months and years to think about what they did and wish they had stopped themselves and done some thinking before they did it. Not only are they locked up in a terrible place, many prisoners have to live with the fact that they caused other people to suffer horribly — victims they purposely attacked or those who were hurt, or even killed, because they accidentally got in the way. Other victims are the people who grieve for friends and family members who were hurt or killed.

- What causes people to act without considering the consequences:
- Extreme anger coupled with the impulsive urge to get even.
- Enjoying the thrill of feeling powerful by bullying or baiting someone.
- Losing contact with reality and the ability to use judgment by using alcohol or drugs.
- Taking a dare.
- Not being able to refuse pressure from a person or a group to hurt someone, steal something, have sex, drink alcohol, take drugs, etc.

All of these have caused prison terms for assault, murder, manslaughter, rape, and theft. They have also caused pain, injury, death, trauma, unwanted pregnancies, poverty, and fear.

These consequences aren't planned. Few people intend to mess up their lives or the lives of others. But when things go wrong they ask, "How did this happen?" Many look for excuses or someone else to blame. But the truth is that they made it happen and if they are honest with themselves they know it. It is also true that the terrible outcomes of their actions wouldn't have happened if, at first, they had found the courage to stop and consider the consequences.

Defuse Hostility

Ideas to Consider #3

One of the most difficult situations to face is being confronted by a hostile person who is yelling threats and insults at you.

There could be lots of different reasons the person is so upset and acting in such an aggressive manner. Whether the reason makes sense or not the person's hostility is beyond reason. Perhaps you did something to offend him or her and maybe you didn't even realize it. Or perhaps you didn't do something the person thought you had promised to do. Maybe he or she is actually angry at someone else, but is taking it out on you instead. It could be that the person is jealous or envious of you or maybe you remind the person of someone he or she doesn't like. Perhaps you offended the person in the past and he or she has held a grudge. The grudge may even be against someone in your family, or a friend, but you're the target. Maybe you didn't respond to a demand the person made the way he or she expected and now the person is trying to punish you.

People who behave in these ways are often individuals who generally feel left out and not cared about by anyone. Some are treated badly by people in their families or neighborhoods. And some are just demanding — wanting what they want when they want it.

So, how do you defuse a hostile person who is in your face? Here are some suggestions to follow if you want to avoid violence:

- Stay cool. Don't do anything at first except breathe deeply. This gives you time to think.
- Look at the person calmly and keep breathing. Don't show fear and don't argue or try to explain anything. Extremely upset people can't hear a word you're saying. If you argue you will inflame not defuse the person and violence may result.
- Try to understand. Respectfully ask, "I can see that you are very upset. What did I do? Tell me what's wrong."
- Then listen and listen some more. Let the person know you understand by repeating in an even voice what you heard him or her say. (For example: "You're angry because I got the last hamburger.")
- No matter how unreasonable you believe the person is being, sincerely express regret and concern. For example: "Oh, I see what you mean. Bummer. It's too bad that happened." If you think it's appropriate, apologize.
- Stop talking and let the person make the next move. By now the person will probably feel much less hostile if he or she believes you understand and care.
- Back off, keeping eye contact. Hold up your head but keep a plain expression.

Refuse the Bait

Ideas to Consider #4

What do bullies want? They want respect but will settle for fear. Bullies may seem strong and scary but it's all an act. They are trying to convince you that they could do you damage, but mainly they are trying to convince themselves. Inside, bullies feel anything but strong. But by scaring and hurting other people they fool themselves into thinking they are proving their strength.

Bullies act like they can damage you because they have been damaged. They have been victims of bad treatment probably as small children. Many were abused and may not remember it. Some still live with abusive people in their homes or neighborhoods. Being hurt causes many people to want to hurt back and not to care who they hurt.

Bullies want to feel powerful so much they don't play fair. They tease or bait you by calling you names, or calling someone you care about names. They accuse you of being (scared, dumb, ugly, chicken, gay, a goody goody, etc.), or take something from you but only when they have the advantage like when they are in a group of bullies or if they have a weapon. Bullies hit below the belt any way they can to sucker you into a fight you are unlikely to win. They do it to get a power high.

When the deck is stacked against you what can you do to try to end the episode without becoming the victim of violence and without groveling? Here are some suggestions:

- First and foremost: Don't take the bait! This means don't argue, trade insults, or try to reason with the bully.
- Show respect (what the bully really wants); don't show fear.
- Breathe and gaze calmly at the bully. If the bully demands you give him or her your money or something else hold your dignity and say something like: "Aw come on, (Jack). You're no thief."
- Slowly walk away keeping eye contact. (Later you might want to anonymously report the incident to your school's administrators if it happened at school.)

Three other ideas:

- Agree. (Imagine the bully has just called you "stupid." Your response, with a smile: "Yep. You may be right. But I do my best.") Then walk away.
- Give them what they want. If more than one grabs your sweater and throws it back and forth baiting you to try to get it, don't. Just say, "If you like it so much, you can have it." This ends the game and they are likely to throw the sweater where you can get it later.
- If a bully without a gang or a weapon hits you this might be the time to respond physically. Surprise the bully with a fast, hard jab. This is the only language some bullies understand. With some there may be more hitting but after that they leave you alone.

Handle the Pressure

Ideas to Consider #5

To "just say no" may sound easy when someone, or a group, is pressuring you to do something you don't want to do. But sometimes it's not so easy.

Let's imagine a situation that involves "peer pressure" and look at ideas for handling it:

Your friends know your parents are going out of town for the weekend and they want to come to your house for a party. They told you that they took some of their parent's liquor and plan to bring it. They also plan to invite some people who like to have sex at parties. You can foresee a bad scene including damage to your house and punishment from your parents when they find out as you know they will. How do you let your friends know you don't want to go along with the plan without having them reject you.

- Create an excuse: Tell them your grandmother (or some other adult relative) is going to spend the weekend at your house while your parents are gone. No way can the party happen then.
- Tell them the first level of truth: Explain that your neighbors see everything and report it. Let them know your parents will find out for sure and ground you for months if you have the party.
- Tell them the next level of truth: Let's say your friends accept what you told them but later on they want you to go to a party they are planning somewhere else. You know there will be alcohol and some of the same people there. You aren't interested but they keep pressuring you to join in. This may be when you are finally ready to explain: "I really like hanging out with you guys. We do a lot of things together that I want to keep doing but that kind of party just isn't my thing. I hope you can accept that." You may have to do this more than once.
- Finally, stand your ground and be true to yourself: If your friends won't leave you alone and keep putting on the pressure this may be when you finally have to say no.

Resolve Problems with Mediation

Ideas to Consider #6

Mediation is a process that is being used more and more in practically every community in many nations including our own. In fact, nations that otherwise might go to war are solving their problems with each other through mediation. It's possible your school has a Peer Mediation Program. (If not, you might help to get one by talking about it with counselors and teachers.)

Here's how it works: Let's say two students are in a heated dispute with one another. It could be about anything. The mediator goes with them to a private place and they work on the problem with the mediator's help until a solution both can live with has been reached. The mediator calls the shots.

- First, the mediator gets both students to agree to these rules:

  1. Whatever we say here is private — it stays in this room.
  2. There will be no interruptions, name calling, put downs, or fighting.
  3. When it's your turn to speak be as honest as you can.
  4. Agree to find a resolution to the conflict.

- Second, the mediator gives each student a turn to tell the other what he or she did that made each one angry.
- Third, the mediator makes sure that each student heard the other correctly by having them take turns telling each other what they heard each other say.
- Fourth, the mediator has each student take a turn to tell the other at least two things that he or she likes or respects about the other.
- Fifth, the mediator has each student take a turn to tell the other what he or she wants the other to do differently that would solve the problem for him or her.
- Sixth, the mediator continues to help the students come up with more ideas they both can agree to in order to solve the problem. This continues until at least one idea for a solution that both students are okay with has been agreed upon.
- Last, the mediator has both students write down the solution using the exact same words. Both sign each other's paper. Finally, the students are asked to shake hands.

Chill Yourself Out

Ideas to Consider #7

Most violence happens because at least one person was extremely angry, unable to think, got out of control, and acted on impulse. It's a chain reaction that can lead to pain and regret.

You can't stop yourself from getting extremely angry or scared at times. That's normal. It's also normal to feel like striking back at whoever or whatever made you upset. But that's not being strong; it's the opposite. It takes great strength and self control to stop yourself and if you can do it, you will give yourself a big advantage. The fact is that it's hard to think when you're upset, but think you must for things to work out right. So, you also need to chill yourself out.

Here are some ways that successful people use to calm down and get back in control of themselves:

- **Breathe!** Are you aware that whenever people become extremely tense they practically stop breathing? This isn't good because when oxygen to the brain is reduced it's hard to think. You go blank and that only makes you feel worse. It also makes it easier for your impulses to take over. So, when you are upset, tell yourself to breathe. Take deep breaths — lots of them. You'll notice a difference soon in how you feel. Your ability to think and handle yourself will return. You will feel your real strength.
- **Count!** Count to ten. This suggestion made by Thomas Jefferson; its worked for millions of people for two centuries. Or you could count backwards from ten to one, or to 100 by fives. When you try it you'll find that it will keep your impulses under control and afterward you will be more able to think straight. Breathe deeply at the same time.
- **Use words that suit you.** Many people prefer to say things to themselves while they breathe deeply instead of counting. Try saying: "You're cool." ... "Chill out now." ... "You're in control." ... "Re - lax."

If you feel like you're about to explode no matter how hard you try to calm yourself down do it so you won't get into trouble and cause yourself to feel regret later. Scream into a pillow. Punch a mattress. Go for a hard run. Go somewhere completely private and talk out loud to yourself about how you feel. Find a friend you trust and talk it out. And don't forget: counselors are people who can be very helpful at times like these.

A Time I Considered the Consequences
A Circle Session

Objectives:

— to allow students to acknowledge the benefits of considering the consequences of acting on angry impulse before doing so

— to acknowledge themselves and each other for using self control.

After setting the tone and reviewing the ground rules, introduce the topic in your own words:

Our topic for this session is 'A Time I Considered the Consequences.' Have you ever noticed how actions almost always bring reactions? Even the simplest greeting from one person draws out a return greeting from the one greeted. Angry words, insults and physical aggression are the same only they usually escalate and get worse as actions and reactions go on and on. Smart people are aware of this. They consider what will happen if they do this or say that and they will stop escalation of a conflict on purpose even though they might feel like getting even. If you decide to take a turn in this session tell us about a time when you

stopped yourself from doing what you felt like doing and used your ability to think about the consequences instead. Tell us how you were feeling at first, what you thought the consequences might be if you acted on those feelings, and what you finally did, but don't tell us who else was involved. The topic is: 'A Time I Considered the Consequences.'

After each circle member who wishes to speak has had a chance, conduct a review to reinforce listening skills (if time allows).

Summary Discussion Questions:

— *What kinds of feelings and impulses did most or all of us have in these situations?*

— *What kinds of consequences would have resulted if the impulses had been acted on?*

— *How do you feel about yourself now for using self control?*

A Time I Chilled Myself Out

A Circle Session

Objective:

— to allow students to exchange information about methods for calming themselves down after becoming extremely stressed by anger or fear.

After setting the tone and reviewing the ground rules, introduce the topic in your own words:

We have been taking a look at some of the toughest things we can face and how to handle ourselves in these situations. The situations we discussed can cause tremendous anger or fear — difficult emotions to bear. Being able to release these feelings and move on is hard, but it can be done. Our topic is about how we can help ourselves do it. The topic is, 'A Time I Chilled Myself Out.' If you decide to speak in this session tell us about a time you were very angry or scared and how you helped yourself get over these feelings by doing something that chilled you out. Maybe you remembered to breathe deeply, count to ten, talked yourself into a calm state of mind, went for a run, danced, etc. We'd like to know how well you think it worked now that you look back on it. The topic is: 'A Time I Chilled Myself Out.'

After each circle member who wishes to speak has had a chance, conduct a review to reinforce listening skills (if time allows).

Summary Discussion Questions:

— Other people can be very helpful at times like these, but who is always available to you for helping you calm down after becoming angry or scared?

— What kinds of methods for chilling out seemed to work best for most of us?

— Did you get any good ideas for ways to help yourself chill out in the future from this session?

PEACE AND HARMONY CAN BE CREATED!

OVERVIEW . . .

As we have seen to our shock and dismay extreme anger fueled by feelings of alienation and castigation are often the root cause of destructive violence in our schools. Walls students build around their "in groups" coupled with shunning and outright cruel treatment of other students who are "different" can create deep resentment and hatred in those shut out and targeted for ridicule. At best this fragmentation and unkindness hurts and leaves lifelong scars. At worst it leads to tragic vengeful acts.

This final unit is concerned with providing students the means for removing the walls themselves and replacing them with bridges where they can see themselves in one another. It is about creating constructive bonds and relationships where they explore commonalities, learn to appreciate each others' unique qualities, and characteristics and to affirm one another. The overall goal is to build a common vision of community made strong because of its diverse population where every student feels a sense of belonging and self worth.

Engaging in these activities, therefore, accomplishes two purposes: it helps to create a healthy and productive learning environment and it helps to prevent destructive behavior. Specifically, this instructional unit has been designed to promote the following understandings about how to create peace and harmony within the classroom and school:

- Everyone at school has an impact on the environment. You can choose to make that impact positive and constructive or negative and destructive.

- If you care about yourself and others you will choose to make a positive impact at school. There are many practical ways to contribute to creating a peaceful and harmonious environment.

- Being kind and generous to others can bring rewards to both givers and receivers. Kindness and generosity promote self respect.

- Unkindness does not promote self respect. Its effect on victims causes pain. It can also promote the urge for vengeance causing even greater misery for more people.

- Human beings are both alike and different at the same time. True understanding of this principle promotes appreciation of self and others. Lack of understanding allows individuals to discount the gift of their own uniqueness and to fear or repudiate diversity in others.

- Some reasons people avoid others are reasonable while many others are unreasonable.

- If you are avoided because of personal characteristics you can't or wouldn't change the best attitude is to consider it the problem, and loss, of those who are avoiding you.

- If you are avoided because of actions that others are justifiably not attracted to, consider changing those actions.

- If you are using unjustifiable reasons to avoid others dismiss those reasons. Instead, act to develop friendly relations with those people.

- Sincerely affirming others and being affirmed by others can significantly boost everyone's morale.

- Forgiving others, letting go of grudges, and forgiving oneself help to create peace and harmony.

- As more and more people want peace and harmony and have the courage and skill to make it happen, it will!

Important resources for the development of this unit and excellent sources of additional information and ideas:

- *Character Education in America's Schools* by Terri Akin, M.S., Gerry Dunne, Ph.D., Susanna Palomares, M.A., and Dianne Schilling, M.S., Carson, California: Innerchoice Publishing Company, 1995. Phone: (310) 816-3085.

- *Helping Teens Stop Violence: A Practical Guide for Counselors, Educators, and Parents* by Allen Creighton, Battered Women's Alternatives and Paul Kivel, Oakland Men's Project, Alameda, California: Hunter House, Inc., Publishers, 1992. Phone: (510) 865-5282.

- *Learning the Skills of Peacemaking: A K - 6 Activity Guide on Resolving Conflict, Communicating, Cooperating* by Naomi Drew, Carson, California: Jalmar Press, 1995. Phone: (310) 816-3085.

- *Peace Patrol: Creating a New Generation of Problem Solvers and Peacemakers* by Eden Steele, Carson, California: Innerchoice Publishing Company, 1994. Phone: (310) 816-3085.

- *The Peaceful Classroom in Action: A K - 6 Activity Guide on How to Create One and How to Keep It!* by Naomi Drew, Carson, California: Jalmar Press, 1999. Phone: (310) 816-3085.

A Place with People Where I Feel Peaceful and Content
A Circle Session

Objective:

— to enable the students to identify the elements in familiar social environments that create peace and harmony. These elements may then be referred to as the other activities in this unit are experienced.

After setting the tone and reviewing the ground rules, introduce the topic in your own words:

We are beginning a new unit in our program today called, 'Peace and Harmony Can Be Created!' Our first activity in the unit is this circle session and our topic is, 'A Place with People Where I Feel Peaceful and Content.' You can probably think of many places in nature where you feel at peace. But for this session think about places where you have been where other people were present and you felt safe and happy. It could have been a place you were in some time ago. Or maybe it's a place you go to now and then — perhaps even more often than that. If you decide to take a turn

describe the place and the circumstances — what goes on there and what makes it so agreeable. Again, the topic is: 'A Place with People Where I Feel (or Felt) Peaceful and Content.'

After each circle member who wishes to speak has had a chance, conduct a review to reinforce listening skills (if time allows).

Summary Discussion Questions:

— *What kinds of things were the people doing and how did they act in most, or all, of the places we described?*

— *Did most, or all, of us seem to feel included with the people in these places — like we belonged and were of value?*

— *As someone else described their place could you see it in your mind's eye?*

PEACE AND HARMONY ON THE WAY!
Individual Writing, Task Groups and Discussion
A Fundamental Activity

Note to teachers and counselors:

This first activity in this unit focuses on how students, faculty and others can contribute to the creation of an improved harmonious and peaceful social atmosphere at school. For maximum positive school-wide outcomes it is recommended that this activity be conducted in as many classrooms as possible throughout the school. This will not only lead to the creation of peace and harmony in those classrooms but also to improved relations among all of the school's stakeholders — everyone! An excellent follow up school-wide project would be the formation of an ad hoc committee of students, faculty and parents to tally the suggestions made in all classrooms and to present the top ten to the assembled student body, faculty and parents.

The purpose of this activity is to encourage students to feel the responsibility of stakeholders and to care more about their classroom and school environments. As a result of participating in these processes the students are also likely to understand more fully their own impact on others and choose to make that impact positive.

Description:

The students idnetify things in the classroom that aggravate them and that could realistically be changed or eliminated without naming names. Then they identify things that could realistically be added to the classroom that would make it more peaceful and harmonious. As a class, they select three to five items from each category and brainstorm how these things could be changed/eliminated and added, and who would be responsible for those actions. The teacher/counselor challenges him/herself and the students to commit to the actions generated by the students. In the second part of this activity this process is repeated using the entire school as the focus.

Objectives:

Students will:

— individually contemplate and write notes to themselves regarding elements in their classroom and school that they would like to see eliminated, changed or added to increase peace and harmony.

— express and listen to varied responses of peers and contribute to generating a group list of ways to create improved classroom and school peace and harmony.

— brainstorm practical actions and who (roles) might undertake those actions with the class.

— understand that their commitment to the actions the class generates will have a positive impact on the classroom and school.

Time needed:

Four 45 to 60 minute class sessions. The first two class sessions focus on the classroom with the second class session immediately following the first. The third and fourth class sessions occur later with the school as the focus. The fourth session should immediately follow the third.

Materials needed:

Writing materials for each student, A copy of the chart following this activity prepared on the board or large chart paper

Directions:

Part One

1. Briefly provide an explanation of this activity by telling the students that they are going to be asked their opinions about how their classroom could be improved by making it a more peaceful and harmonious place. Explain that after they have focused on the classroom their opinions will be sought regarding the school as whole. Point out that their opinions will be taken seriously.

2. Ask the students to take out writing materials for some brief notes they will write to themselves. Then explain that their opinions about what is not agreeable about the classroom will be the first focus. Ask: *What things in this classroom that could be changed or eliminated bother you and make the classroom less peaceful and harmonious than it could be? Think of aggravating circumstances or situations that are not pleasant for you. (Jokingly:) Don't list me because I'm here to stay, but if I do something completely unnecessary that you'd like me to do differently or stop doing you can list that. If other people come to mind, don't list them by name. Just describe what it is they do that you would like to have them change or stop doing. An example of something you might list would be no more shouting as we come into the room before class starts.*

3. Assist the students to form task groups of no more than four members per group. (You may wish to use existing cooperative learning groups, or formulate new ones. If this latter course is taken guide them through a process of determining roles: leader, recorder, process consultant, encourager, etc.)

4. Ask the task groups to talk among themselves and share the opinions they personally listed that they would be comfortable sharing. Explain that their challenge is to reach consensus in generating a group list of three to five opinions. Be sure each group has a recorder to accomplish this. Do not circulate among the groups in order to allow them privacy for expressing their thoughts without the possible inhibitions or embarrassment your presence might cause. If, however, a group is in obvious distress intervene to lend a hand.

5. Guide the reporting of the groups' opinions. Call the attention of the class to the chart. Restate the challenge you gave the students and call on the recorder in each group to read the opinions their groups generated. As each recorder reads his/her list, chart each statement. As statements are replicated make check marks beside the first one to indicate repetitions.

6. Repeat steps 2 through 5 with this change of focus. Ask: *What would you like to see added to the classroom that could realistically be added that would make it more peaceful and harmonious? An example might be playing a CD with soft music or nature sounds whenever we are doing independent work or work in pairs.*

7. After the groups' opinions regarding what could be added to the classroom that would make it more peaceful and harmonious have been charted, suggest: *Let's pick out three to five of the statements in each of these two categories and brainstorm how they might be done.* Chart the students' ideas for actions that could be taken to eliminate/change or add things to make the classroom more harmonious and peaceful.

8. After brainstorming how the ideas could become actions ask the class to identify who the logical person(s) might be to undertake those actions. Chart the *roles* of these individuals. For example, if it is suggested that you eliminate, change or add an action, write "teacher" on the chart. If the actions of certain students are targeted for change, elimination or addition, write "some students."

9. It is likely that "teacher" will be listed. Commit to the class to undertake one or more of the suggestions. Be specific. Name each action and tell the class when and how you will do it. Then suggest that they make a commitment to themselves to select one or more of the actions and commit to them.

10. In a few days ask the class if they notice a difference in the level of peace and harmony in the classroom. Guide them through an evaluation process in which they openly discuss how well commitments have been met to create peace and harmony. Regardless of shortcomings, warmly acknowledge the students for the contributions they have made.

Part Two:

Repeat Part One with the school as the focus. Create a new chart with the title, "How To Make Our School More Peaceful and Harmonious."

Extension for all grades:

Challenge the students to analyze the ways in which they can help to bring peace and harmony to their families by starting with themselves (the only family member over whom they actually have control). Suggest they write down the things they know they could stop and start doing to help create a peaceful and harmonious home. Point out that if they take this seriously and stick to it for at least a week no matter how hard it might be at times they may be very pleasantly surprised with the results and the appreciation they receive. Best of all, creating peace and harmony wherever we find ourselves rewards each of us with increased self respect and self esteem.

HOW TO MAKE OUR CLASSROOM MORE PEACEFUL AND HARMONIOUS

CHANGE OR ELIMINATE:	HOW?	WHO?

ADD:	HOW?	WHO?

KINDNESS CAN BRING REWARDS

Listening to Fables, Discussion, Research, and Student Presentations — A Fundamental Activity

Note to teachers and counselors:

The fables summarized in this activity are from Section Four, "Easing the Path," of *The Moral Compass: Stories for a Life's Journey* by William J. Bennett (Simon & Schuster, Publisher, 1995). William Bennett also served as editor for *The Book of Virtues* (Simon & Schuster, 1993). Stories from these or other books can be used with follow up discussions as suggested here to provide examples and principles for how to create peace and harmony through kindness. This activity may also be repeated with different stories after several months as a "booster."

The purposes of this activity are to provide a stimulus to students' understanding of the value of human kindness and the rewards it can bring to both givers and receivers, as well as the emptiness and torment that can result from being unkind, and, second, while these principles are generally true, this activity also allows students to examine and discuss complexities in motivation and outcomes of kind and unkind behavior.

Description:

Three fables are read, or told, to the students with discussion after each one to determine the moral or lesson offered. Next, students are challenged to conduct research into literature and history to locate and analyze fictional stories and nonfictional accounts of human kindness as well as stories of misery resulting from human greed and cruelty.

Objectives:

Students will:

— listen to three fables and discuss their meaning.
— find and analyze a fictional story or nonfictional account of human kindness or unkindness with one or two partners.
— prepare and present a report to the class about the story they found and lead a class discussion regarding its meaning.

Time needed:

Three 40 to 60 minute class sessions. The first class session focuses on the fables and discussions. The second may be spent in beginning research or later in planning presentations. The students present their stories to the class in the third class session.

Materials needed:

Optional: a copy of *The Moral Compass* where the original versions of the fables in this activity may be found along with many others. The three stories begin on these pages in *The Moral Compass*: "The

Princess Who Wanted to Be Beautiful" - page 365; "Mr. Straw" - page 370; and "The Mouse Tower" - page 424. Other sources of similar fables and stories may be researched by the students in the library and on the internet.

Directions:

Part One

1. Set the tone for this activity by telling the students that you would like to read (or tell) them three stories called fables. Look up "fable" and "moral" in the dictionary and/or discuss what they may already know: a fable is a fictitious story in which talking animals are often the main characters. A fable is told to convey a point about how to understand the human condition and/or to live life in harmony with oneself and others — the moral. Explain that at the end of each fable you will ask them what they believe the moral to be and to think to themselves about how it applies to their own lives.

2. Read the following summaries of fables to the class as presented below, read the fuller versions from *The Moral Compass*, or tell the fables to the class in your own words. Be sure to hold a discussion about each one before going to the next. Discussion questions are offered for each fable.

THE PRINCESS WHO WANTED TO BE BEAUTIFUL

Once upon a time there lived a little princess who was very unhappy because she believed she was not beautiful or even pretty enough to ever become a queen.

One day as she sat in the garden by a wall feeling sorry for herself and crying an old woman walking on a road by the wall heard her and asked why she cried. When she told the woman that she was not beautiful and would probably never be a queen the woman suggested: "Why don't you go out into the world and find someone who can make you beautiful?" And then the woman walked away.

This seemed like such a good idea to the little princess that she hopped over the wall and sped down the road. (Strangely, the old woman was nowhere to be seen.) Before the little princess had gone very far she came up to a little boy who was painfully stumbling along. He touched her sleeve and asked her where she was going.

After she answered his question the boy explained that he was blind and needed her help to find his way home. So the little princess took his hand and walked with him until they came to the cottage beside the road where he lived. Then she hurried on her way because she felt she had lost precious time.

But before she had gone very far the little princess came to a little girl crying beside the road. The girl saw the princess and asked her where she was going. The princess told her and then listened as the girl explained that her mother was very sick and had sent her to the dairy for milk and eggs but since she had no money none was given to her. The little princess quickly reached into her purse and pulled out one of two gold pieces she had brought with her to buy herself food for her journey. She gave it to the girl who was so happy her smile was like sunshine that lighted them both. The little princess hurried off, however, because she felt she had once again taken up too much time and was no more beautiful than she was when she started her journey.

Suddenly the little princess came upon the old woman who she had met that morning. The woman asked if she had done what she suggested. The little princess said "Yes," but added, "I'm still ugly."

Immediately the woman said, "Oh no, you aren't" and brought out a mirror. As she looked at herself in the mirror the little princess saw a strange thing: her eyes, in leading the blind boy, had grown as bright as stars and her hair shined like the gold piece she gave to the girl.

"Will I ever be a queen?" the little princess asked.

At that the old woman brought out a crown from her bundle and placed it on her head. "You are a queen, my dear!" she said.

Discussion Questions:

— *What were some of the qualities the little princess showed?* (courage, kindness, generosity)

— *What is the moral of this fable?* (William Bennett states: In the end there are few things more beautiful than a kind heart. Another message: Sometimes life gives us unexpected opportunities we weren't looking for to benefit others and ourselves.)

— *Did the little princess realize that she was benefitting herself by being kind to others?* (No, she was simply and spontaneously kind.)

MR. STRAW — An Ancient Tale from Japan

Once upon a time there lived a poor man who had no luck and as a result he had no home, wife or children. He was so thin from hunger that he was like a piece of straw and that's how he got his name.

Each day he went to the temple to ask the Goddess of Fortune for some luck and one day he heard a voice that told him that the first thing he touched after leaving the temple would bring him great good fortune.

Amazed, Mr. Straw hurried out of the temple but he was so excited he tripped on the temple steps and fell to the bottom. When he got up out of the dirt he found that his hand was clutching a piece of straw which he decided not to throw away because the Goddess must have wanted him to have and keep it.

As he walked a dragonfly came at him again and again buzzing incessantly. At first he shooed it but then decided to tie it to the straw. As he walked along it looked like a tiny kite on a string.

Soon he came upon the flower lady and her little boy. The boy was tired of walking and feeling grumpy, but when the boy saw Mr. Straw's dragonfly kite he became excited and asked his mother if he could have it. Before she could reply Mr. Straw gave it to the boy because he knew it would cheer up the little fellow. The flower lady was so impressed by his gift that she gave Mr. Straw a rose in payment.

After thanking her Mr. Straw went on his way and then saw a very forlorn looking young man sitting on a tree stump near the road. He looked so sad that Mr. Straw asked him what was wrong.

"I'm going to ask my girlfriend to marry me this evening but I'm so poor that I have no gift to give her," responded the young man. Mr. Straw sympathized and said he was poor too. Then he offered the young man his rose which the man was very pleased to accept for his girlfriend. "All I can give you for it are these three oranges," he said. Mr. Straw took the oranges which were plump and juicy.

Just then a peddler came along pulling his cart. "Can you help me?" he asked Mr. Straw. "I need a drink of water. I'm so thirsty from pulling this cart all day." Mr. Straw explained that there were no wells nearby but offered the poor man his oranges because they contained so much juice. The grateful peddler reached into his cart and pulled out a beautiful roll of silk which he gave to Mr. Straw in return for his kindness.

As Mr. Straw proceeded down the road with the silk under his arm a princess in a golden carriage came toward him. The princess saw the silk and ordered the carriage stopped. She asked Mr. Straw where he got it. "It's perfect for my father's birthday," she said. "I want to make him a new royal robe."

"You may take it since it's his birthday," said Mr. Straw to the delighted princess who couldn't believe her luck. In return she gave Mr. Straw a beautiful jewel.

At that point Mr. Straw took the jewel and sold it to a merchant for a large sum of money. He spent the money on a great rice field which he worked very hard. His work paid off with a large crop. Each year he bought more land and reaped an even greater rice crop. He became a rich man.

But did this change Mr. Straw? No. He shared his rice with hungry people. He built a school for the children of the village and always helped anyone in need. The legend everyone told was that his luck came from a piece of straw, but Mr. Straw knew differently.

Discussion Questions:

— *Where do you think Mr. Straw knew his luck came from?* (Mr. Straw knew it came from his kindness.)

— *What happened inside Mr. Straw each time he saw someone in need?* (He understood, empathized, and wanted to make each person feel better.)

— *What is the moral of this story?* (William Bennett states: Mr. Straw...quite intentionally raises himself by lifting a hand to help others.)

THE MOUSE TOWER — A Medieval Tale from Germany

Hatto, the bishop was known to be rich and greedy. Never did he pray or give alms to the poor. It wasn't enough for Hatto to own the richest farms with granaries fully stocked with wheat and corn. He always wanted more. Again and again he raised the people's taxes. He built a tower of stone on an island in the river Rhine and charged a toll to any boat owner who wanted to pass. As time went by his moneybags were full to overflowing — bursting, in fact. And the people grew poorer and poorer.

One spring the river overflowed and flooded all the farmland ruining the crops and causing famine. The poor, starving people came to Hatto for help and each time they approached his gates he yelled and screamed and sent them away. But the people kept coming because they didn't know what else to do.

Finally Hatto told them to meet him at his largest barn and he would end their suffering. The people gained hope and happiness. They told their children they would finally get something to eat.

That night with hateful eyes Hatto watched the people stumble into the barn. As soon as everyone was inside he shut and bolted the doors. The people waited for Hatto to enter and distribute food but after awhile they heard him laugh and shout, "You have pestered me like rats. Now, like rats, you will die."

The people realized that they had been betrayed and begged to be let out. They pounded on the walls but they were so weak from hunger they couldn't get out. Hatto exclaimed that he had done a good thing ridding the country of rats that would only eat up the food.

But that night Hatto was awakened by rapid scratching sounds like something running across the floor. The next morning he found an expensive portrait of himself that he loved shredded to bits. He could see the marks made by rat's teeth. And a few days later he found out that rats had eaten all the corn in one of the granaries.

Time went by. Days. Weeks. Months. Then finally a servant went to the barn and opened the door. It was empty!

More and more incidents with rats occurred. Rats were everywhere — on Hatto's table at mealtime, in his bed at bedtime, everywhere. They ate all the food in the pantry. Then they went after the wood walls.

One day a servant warned Hatto to get away as quickly as possible. Hatto looked out the window and saw millions of rats swarming for him. He jumped on his horse and beat it brutally to run faster than the rats to the river where he jumped into his boat and rowed for the tower on the island where he had food and money hidden.

Despite the strong current and steep island shores and walls of the tower the squealing rats got onto the island and managed to get inside of the tower. Hatto was frightened to death and climbed the stairs to the uppermost room. In desperation he threw food out of the window hoping to distract and appease the rats but it didn't work. He could hear them chewing down the wooden door that he tried to barricade with everything he could find — bags of wheat and even bags of money.

A few days later Hatto's servants went to the tower. They found the moneybags and some of the food, but there was no sign of Hatto at all.

Discussion Questions:

— *What were some of Hatto's characteristics?* (unkindness, greed, cruelty, merciless- ness, selfishness, heartlessness)

— *Did Hatto ever feel regret for his cruel actions?* (Any regret Hatto may have felt was probably about how things turned out badly for him; he demon- strated no feelings of guilt or remorse for his treatment of the people)

— *What is the moral of this story?* (Justice can be very harsh. Man's cruel inhu- manity to man is tragic and shameful.)

3. Point out: *The morals of these three fables are clear and direct. Kindness will be rewarded and unkindness will be punished. 'The laws of the universe' generally work this way, but sometimes life situations are more complex and puzzling. Sometimes rewards aren't what was hoped for. Some- times people are only kind because they expect a reward. Does that 'count'? Some- times unkind people seem to be the winners when we'd rather see them lose. Sometimes the kindest thing to do for someone is to do nothing because he or she really needs to help him/herself. These are very interesting questions to consider.*

4. Explain the assignment: *There are lots of other stories, both fiction and nonfiction, about kindness and unkindness for us to read, examine, tell each other about, and learn lessons from. In partners or three- somes you will have a chance to find a true story about a real hero, heroine or villain, or a fictional story, perhaps another fable, and present it to the class. You may take turns telling the story and/or acting it out. You may decide to create an illustration to show*

us or you might even find a piece of music that ties in with your story to play for us. After you present your story ask us what the moral or message is and we will discuss it.

Part Two

5. Assist the students to form pairs, or threesomes, and to begin their research. Excellent additional stories for this purpose are offered in the section of *The Moral Compass* entitled, "Easing the Path." The "Chicken Soup" books are also an excellent source. Leads to other stories, particularly biographies, may be found in the library or on the internet. You may lead the class in a brief brain- storming activity to generate key words for this purpose including: kindness, unkindness, compassion, motivation, empathy, justice, retribution, etc. (You may wish to approve each story chosen by the students to make sure it ties in sufficiently well with the general theme of this activity.)

Part Three

6. The students make their presentations to the class. Intervene only when needed to add clarification to the stories or to help with discussions centering on their meaning. Lead an applause at the end of each presentation.

Extension for all grade levels:

Arrange for your students to present their stories and dramatizations as well as follow up discussions about the morals of the stories to classes of younger students.

A Time I Showed Someone Who was Feeling Bad that I Cared
A Circle Session

Objectives:

— to enable students to gain reinforcement for caring behavior

— to describe the ways they demonstrated support and caring for others.

After setting the tone and reviewing the ground rules, introduce the topic in your own words:

Our topic for this circle session is: 'A Time I Showed Someone Who was Feeling Bad that I Cared.' We all know how much it means when you're feeling terrible about something and a friend comes along and gives support. Think about a time when you were the one who did this. Perhaps a recent example comes to mind of how you stood by someone who was hurting and let him, or her, know you understood and cared about his, or her, feelings. Or perhaps you remember a situation like this some time back. If you take a turn tell us what the person was upset about if you think it would be appropriate but don't tell us who it was. Most important, be sure to tell us what you said and did. Our topic is: 'A Time I Showed Someone Who was Feeling Bad that I Cared.'

After each circle member who wishes to speak has had a chance, conduct a review to reinforce listening skills (if time allows).

Summary Discussion Questions:

— *What were some of the words and actions that we used to be supportive of someone who is feeling bad?*

— *How did the people who were hurting generally seem to feel about the caring we tried to show?*

— *As you look back on what you did how does it make you feel about yourself?*

I Helped Someone Who Needed and Wanted My Help

A Circle Session

Objectives:

— to allow students to identify and describe truly helpful actions.

— students will be enabled to consider when it is best to offer a hand to someone and when it's better to allow someone to solve his, or her, own problem.

After setting the tone and reviewing the ground rules, introduce the topic in your own words:

Our topic for this circle session is: 'I Helped Someone Who Needed and Wanted My Help.' You can probably think of times when someone needed help but wouldn't accept it when it was offered. Likewise, times may come to mind when someone wanted help but you knew it was better for him, or her, to be responsible for his, or her, own problem. But then there are times when people really need and want help and those are the situations we are focusing on in this session. Can you remember offering to help someone in those circumstances who

accepted your help? If you speak in this session don't tell us who it was, but do tell us about the situation, how you offered your help, and what you did to be helpful. The topic is: 'I Helped Someone Who Needed and Wanted My Help.'

After each circle member who wishes to speak has had a chance, conduct a review to reinforce listening skills (if time allows).

Summary Discussion Questions:

— *Why is it important to offer to help someone before you just start doing what you think would be helpful?*

— *How did the people we helped seem to feel about it?*

— *How do you feel about yourself now as you recall what you did to be helpful to someone?*

HOW DIFFERENT ARE WE REALLY?

Experiment, Brainstorming, Teacher/Counselor Presentation, and Discussion — A Fundamental Activity

The purpose of this activity is to provide students with a new way of looking at differences that exist between them which highlights how, as human beings, they are individually unique and fundamentally alike at the same time. Students are also encouraged to understand how differences in people can cause them to be seen as intimidating or unworthy on the one hand or as interesting and stimulating on the other. They are also encouraged to form relationships with others who are "different" from them in order to enrich their own lives.

Description:

Part One

The students are each offered a small rock from a bag of rocks as they enter the classroom. They are asked to "get to know it," name it, and introduce it to other students' rocks. Next, all of the rocks are placed back in the bag and spilled out onto a surface. Then the students are invited to find their own rocks. Discussion about the principle of the uniqueness of all things follows.

Part Two

The students are asked to brainstorm human characteristics that are the same and then to brainstorm human characteristics that are different. "The Principle of Unity and Diversity" paradox is presented by the teacher/counselor who leads a discussion about the implications of both parts of this activity for enhancing or curtailing relationships with oneself and others.

Objectives:

Students will:

— participate in an experiment in which they discover the uniquenesses in objects that are usually seen as the same.

— brainstorm ways in which human beings are the same and different and then consider how the "differences" become similarities when considered from a broader perspective.

— listen to a teacher/counselor presentation and discuss how one's attitude about human similarities and differences may result in negative or positive outcomes.

Time needed:

One full class period

Materials needed:

A bag containing enough small rocks for every student to have one (peanuts or lemons may be substituted) and a prepared chalkboard or chart as shown:

How People are the Same:	How People are Different:

Directions:

Part One: The Experiment

1. As the students enter the classroom meet them at the door with a bag of small rocks and offer each one a rock. When they ask what the rock is for tell them: *Get to know your rock. Give it a name and introduce him or her to the other rocks that have been adopted by the other students. Have fun!*

2. Call the class to order. Keeping explanations to a minimum at this point, direct the students to place their rocks back into the bag. Spill the collected rocks out onto a surface — a tabletop or the floor — and invite small groups of students to come and find their own rocks one group at a time. (All rocks will be reunited with their owners probably with much fanfare and jubilation.)

3. Discuss the meaning of the activity by asking:

— *Before you found your rock did you feel confident that you would be able to do it?*

— *Why were you confident and why did you succeed?*

— *Had you ever thought of 'ordinary' rocks as having lots of individual characteristics before?*

— *Let's transfer what we've learned about our ability to get to know rocks, to our ability to get to know people, especially when we group people in our minds into categories like racial and ethnic categories, or age categories, or groups of students at school. Are members of these categories really all alike?*

— *Why is it important to remember that each person is unique like the rocks we've made friends with?*

Part Two: Brainstorming, Charting, and Discussion

4. Present the chart headings to the students and point to the first part. Ask them to brainstorm all the ways they can think of in which all people are exactly the same. As the students name the similarities chart them. Examples: "All are born of two parents." "All live on the planet Earth." "All have the same basic body structure." "All have feelings." "All will die." Etc.

5. Next, point to the second part of the chart and ask the students to name ways in which people are different. Chart their statements. Examples: "Color of skin." "Cultures." "Languages." "Intelligence." Etc.

6. Offer this challenge: *Let's think about the differences in a new way with a larger perspective.* Start with the first example of a way in which the students stated that people are different and ask if all people share some type of this characteristic. For example: *We may have different colors of skin, but do we all have a skin color?* When the students say yes, elaborate: *Correct, and in that way we are the same, right?* Then draw a circle around the item and an arrow from it to the other side of the chart that lists the ways in which people are the same.

7. Continue in this manner with each characteristic. Here are more examples: *We have different cultures, but do we all have a culture? We may speak different languages, but do we all have a language?*

Some of us may be smarter than others, but does everyone have some intelligence? Etc.

8. Ask: *Does this tell us that even in the ways that we are different we are also the same?* Discuss how many ways people may seem different but are actually alike.

9. Present the following information:

We've had two activities — one with rocks that pointed out how different each of us is from everyone else and another activity with these two lists which pointed out how much alike all human beings are. One activity tells us one thing and the other tells us the opposite. Is this confusing? Actually it's a mystery, a paradox — a reality that is true yet contradicts itself. For centuries the best minds have been fascinated with this paradox which is called 'The Principle of Unity and Diversity.' The principle states that humans are both alike and different at the same time.

This principle can be used by each person to make their relationships with themselves and others enjoyable. When it is not understood it can make a person's relationships lifeless or even miserable. If you don't realize that everyone is unique and yet the same at the same time you miss a lot. You can look at yourself and not realize how unique and valuable you are and what a gift that is. And you can look at others, like groups of a particular race, or culture, or groups at school and see them as all the same and scary, or stuck up, or not as valuable as the group you belong to. If you do that you fail to understand that they are just as human as you are and you miss out on getting to know them as individuals like you got to know your rock. And if you avoid people because of this you also miss out on the fun of experiencing their group's characteristics which might be very interesting.

10. Bring in the students at this point. Spark discussion by asking: *How do you think understanding and appreciating 'The Principle of Unity and Diversity' can make your relationship with yourself and others enjoyable?* (These are the opposite of those stated in item 9, above.) Listen to the students' responses and acknowledge them for their insights.

11. Finally, challenge the students to make an effort to get to know people who are "different" from them because doing so makes life so much more interesting. It also contributes to creating peace and harmony for ourselves and others.

I Made Friends with Someone Who's Different from Me

A Circle Session

Objectives:

— to reinforce students for creating friendly relationships with others who they classify as "different" from themselves in some way

— to encourage them to value the unique characteristics of these friends.

After setting the tone and reviewing the ground rules, introduce the topic in your own words:

Today we are going to focus on relationships. The topic is: 'I Made Friends with Someone Who's Different from Me.' We've been learning that we are all alike and yet completely unique. So all of our friends are different, of course. But for this session think about a good relationship you have created (or co-created) with someone who is obviously different from you in some way. It could be someone of a different race or culture, someone with very different interests from yours, someone older or younger, someone with very different talents from yours, etc. If you decide to take a turn tell us how you became friendly and what your

differences are. Most important, tell us what you appreciate about each other. Our topic is: 'I Made Friends with Someone Who's Different from Me.'

After each circle member who wishes to speak has had a chance, conduct a review to reinforce listening skills (if time allows).

Summary Discussion Questions:

— *Why do you think people often stay away from people who have some obvious differences from them?*

— *Did the differences between ourselves and the people we described cause difficulties in our relationships with them, or did they make the relationships more interesting?*

— *As we got to know these people better what became more important — the similarities or the differences between ourselves and them?*

LOOK INSIDE AND REACH OUT
Teacher/Counselor Presentation, Charting and Discussion
A Fundamental Activity

Note to Teachers and Counselors:

This is a particularly potent and relevant activity. Be sure to do it but be aware that it could spark emotional reactions in students that could embarrass them. For this reason it is important to present a calm and serious manner at all times.

The purpose of this activity is to enable students to understand that many reasons they avoid others and are avoided by others at school are unreasonable while some others are justified. They are also challenged to (1) drop any concerns they may have felt about being avoided for personal characteristics they cannot change even if they wanted to, (2) consider changing actions others justifiably are not attracted to, and (3) dismiss unjustifiable reasons for avoiding certain others and to reach out to them instead.

Description:

The students are asked to consider a series of questions regarding why they might avoid another person at school. They then analyze the reasons first in terms of which are unjustifiable and then which are justifiable. Next, they list the reasons people avoid others that they believe are the most unreasonable. The students are then challenged to use what they have learned to make appropriate changes in their attitudes toward themselves and their behavior toward others.

Objectives:

Students will:

— introspectively examine their attitudes and actions and those of others with respect to avoidance.

— participate in generating lists of unjustifiable and justifiable reasons students avoid others at school.

— discuss healthy attitudes about being the victim of avoidance for unjustifiable reasons.

— listen to a challenge to appropriately change attitudes and behavior.

Time needed:

One full class period

Materials needed:

Three charts on the chalkboard or chart paper with these headings:

Chart One: Characteristics people can't change about themselves or wouldn't want to:

Chart Two: Characteristics people can change and if they did they would probably have friendly relationships with more people:

Chart Three: The most unreasonable reasons for not creating friendly relationships with other people at school:

Directions:

1. Begin this activity by asking the students if they remember "The Principle of Unity and Diversity" that was offered in the former activity and what it means. Here's a summary:

Human beings are both alike and different at the same time. True understanding of this principle promotes appreciation of self and others. Lack of understanding allows individuals to discount the gift of their own uniqueness and to fear or repudiate diversity in others.

2. Explain to the students that you have a series of yes or no questions for them to ask themselves. Suggest they close their eyes and relax as they listen to the questions. Their job is to mentally answer as honestly as they can. Their answers will remain private.

3. When the students are ready tell them: *Think about whether or not there are any people here at school you have nothing to do with. The questions are about their characteristics and your reasons.* Then slowly ask the following questions pausing a few seconds after each one:

— If you don't speak to some people at school and rarely look at them, why is that? Is it because they...

> *...are people you never met and you just don't know them?*
>
> *...act superior and avoided you first?*
>
> *...are male?*
>
> *...are female?*

...are younger than you or if they are your same age seem immature?

...are adults — teachers, administrators, school workers, or parents?

...are just too different in too many ways?

...have a disability?

...are members of a different race or ethnic group?

...are jocks?

...are always using computers?

...are scary or seem to make themselves weird on purpose with the way they talk, dress or act?

...have a different culture?

...have a different religion?

...have different hobbies and interests from yours?"

...are religious?

...aren't religious?

...are too physically developed for their age?

...aren't physically developed enough for their age?

...are from a family with less money than yours?

...are from a family with more money than yours?

4. State: *I mentioned many different characteristics. Ask yourself if you have any of these characteristics? Don't raise your hand. Just be honest with yourself.* At this point you may wish to tell the class in a matter-of-fact manner about some of these characteristics that you have. If you do, select characteristics that you feel good about but may have been avoided for when you were in school. (A revelation of this type is likely to enliven the activity by intriguing or amusing the students.)

5. Call the student's attention to Chart One and point out: *Many of these characteristics are things people can't change about themselves or wouldn't want to. What were some of those unchangeable characteristics in the questions we asked ourselves?* As the students recall these characteristics list them under the chart's heading.

6. When the list is complete, ask:

— *If someone has nothing to do with you because you have some of these characteristics what is the smartest attitude for you to take about it?*

— *Whose problem is it if these kinds of characteristics are held against you?*

7. Call the student's attention to Chart Two and point out: *Some characteristics are within a person's power to change and if they did they would probably have more friendly relationships with more people. There were two characteristics like that in the questions. Do you remember what they were?* As the students recall the two characteristics list them under the chart's heading. (The two characteristics are: (1) people who act superior and avoid you first, and (2) people who are scary or seem to make themselves weird on purpose with the way they talk, dress or act.)

8. Shift gears. Announce: *We've been talking about how we might feel or respond if someone avoids us because certain of characteristics, but now let's turn our thinking around. When I asked you to think about reasons for not speaking to or looking at someone, did you mentally answer yes to some of the reasons? It's not necessary to raise your hand. What is necessary is for you to be honest with yourself.*

9. Point to Chart Three. *Let's make a list of the most unreasonable reasons for not creating friendly relationships with other people at school.* As the students recall the reasons they consider to be the most unreasonable, list them on the chart.

10. Point out the similarities between the lists on Chart One and Chart Three and ask, *Why are these so similar?*

11. Close the activity by telling the students: *I challenge you to do three things for yourself which will also help create peace and harmony in our classroom and school:* (Point to chart One.) *First, never worry about some characteristics you have that you can't change and may not ever want to change that other people don't like. Understand that it's their problem, not yours.* (Point to Chart Two.) *Second, work to change anything about yourself that you could change that would create more friendly relationships with others for you.* (Point to Chart Three.) *Third, stop letting unreasonable reasons stand in the way of your speaking to and looking at other people here at school. Just dismiss those reasons and allow yourself to have more friends.*

I Let Go of a Grudge
A Circle Session

Objective:

— to help students to understand that by letting go of grudges they relieve themselves of emotional burdens.

After setting the tone and reviewing the ground rules, introduce the topic in your own words:

Our topic for this circle session is: 'I Let Go of a Grudge.' We've been focusing recently on how to avoid offending others and how to include them instead of avoiding or hurting them. This session looks at the other side of the coin when you were the victim. All of us have felt hurt, or excluded, or victimized by unkind treatment at one time or another. And many times when this happens what is the best attitude to take? Think of a time when you were able to drop a grudge. It may have been hard right afterward, but at some point you were able to drop it from your heart and mind. Perhaps you even forgave the person who offended you. Don't tell us who it was if you

choose to take a turn. Just describe what happened and how you decided to drop your bad feelings and move on. The topic is: 'I Let Go of a Grudge.'

After each circle member who wishes to speak has had a chance, conduct a review to reinforce listening skills (if time allows).

Summary Discussion Questions:

— *Why can it be so hard to let go of a grudge?*

— *When you hold a grudge against someone are you giving them power over you?*

— *Who generally benefits most when you let go of a grudge?*

— *Just because you let go of a grudge and maybe even forgive someone who offends you, does this mean you are willing to allow yourself to be offended by the person again?*

A Time I Forgave Myself
A Circle Session

Objective:

— to allow students to share their understanding that the best attitude to take toward one's own mistakes is to learn from them and let go of guilty feelings.

After setting the tone and reviewing the ground rules, introduce the topic in your own words:

Today our topic is, 'A Time I Forgave Myself.' In our last circle session we talked about grudges we held against other people and let go of. We may have even forgiven them. This session is about letting go of grudges against ourselves. Did you realize that you can hold a grudge against yourself? Many people do it a lot and make themselves miserable. Such grudges are called 'guilt.' When you have made a mistake and you feel bad about it and forgive yourself it doesn't mean that you will allow yourself to do the same thing again. It just means that you've decided to stop beating yourself up for it. Can you remember a time

when you did that? If you decide to take a turn tell us about the mistake, what you learned from it, and how you let go of your grudge against yourself. The topic is, 'A Time I Forgave Myself.'

After each circle member who wishes to speak has had a chance, conduct a review to reinforce listening skills (if time allows).

Summary Discussion Questions:

— It's been said that mistakes are the best teachers. Do you agree?

— It's also been said that sometimes we are our own worst enemies. Do you agree?

— If you learn from a mistake you've made and then forgive yourself, who benefits?

WHAT I LIKE ABOUT YOU...
Bulletin Board Display Preparation, Writing, and Discussion
A Fundamental Activity

The purpose of this activity is to provide students with the opportunity to exchange positive statements about their likable qualities. This activity will enlighten some students about the power of sincere compliments. Others will receive a significant boost in morale by receiving the compliments. Most students are likely to benefit in both ways.

Description:

A bulletin board is prepared with a banner and photos of students. Students write brief statements about what they like about each other on post-its. Then they adhere their post-its to the bulletin board beside the photos of the students the statements are about. A culminating discussion concludes the activity.

Objectives:

Students will:

— cooperate in preparing a bulletin board with photos and decorations.

— write brief individual statements for as many other students as possible regarding what they like about them.

— discuss the feelings they experience when they give and receive positive personal statements.

Time needed:

Ten minutes to introduce the activity on the first day; an interim time period for gathering photos and preparing the bulletin board; informal time segments for students to prepare and place their post-its on the bulletin board over several days time; and about fifteen minutes for a culminating discussion on the final day

Materials needed:

A bulletin board with a banner saying: "What I Like about You..." that is large enough for photos of all of the students in the class, and room around each photo for at least 15 small post-its; photos of students (cut from the class collection of school photos, photos they bring themselves from home, or photos taken by you with a Polaroid camera); and several packets of 1-1/2 x 2 inch post-its in different colors.

Directions:

1. Introduce the activity: *It always makes people feel good when they know what other people like about them and when you tell someone what you like about him or her it can make you feel good too. In this activity*

we will all get the chance to do this. The activity we will do is a simple one, but very meaningful. We will post a photo of each member of the class on the bulletin board. (Elaborate on the procedure for acquiring the photos that will work best for your class.) *When all of the photos are up you will be given time each day to write individual statements or descriptions on post-its about other students and then you may post them under and around the person's photo. You may also help to decorate the bulletin board as we prepare it.*

2. State the guidelines:

Each statement you make will tell the person whose photo you put it by something you like about him or her. No other messages.

Write the person's name you are writing to at the top of the post-it. Then write, "I like... .

Be brief — there's not much room on these small post-its. You can sign it or put your initials on it if you want to.

Try your best to write a statement for everyone in the class, even students you still don't know very well.

3. Clarify workable time frames for preparing the bulletin board with the photos and posting the positive statements. Be sure to add a photo of yourself and add your post-it statements to the bulletin board about each of the students as well.

4. At least once a day when the students are not in the classroom review the statements on the post-its to make sure all of them are positive. Remove any that are not and make sure all the students have post-its beside their pictures.

5. At the end of the time set for sticking the post-its to the bulletin board, conduct a lighthearted class discussion by asking:

— *How does it make you feel to read all of the statements your classmates made on the post-its telling you what they like about you?*

— *Did you get any interesting pleasant surprises about what someone said they liked about you?*

— *How did it make you feel when you wrote about something you like about someone and placed it by his or her picture?*

— *Did anyone take this a step further and just tell someone in the class what you like about him or her?*

— *Did anyone go even further and tell someone who's not in our class — a friend or family member, perhaps — what you like about him or her?*

— *What does an activity like this achieve?*

6. Thank the students for their contributions which made this activity fun and successful.

EACH OF US CAN PROMOTE PEACE!
Brainstorming Ideas and Creating Posters
A Culminating Activity

The purpose of this activity is to bring closure to this final unit in an enjoyable and creative way. While brainstorming ideas for their posters students will review the concepts and skills they have learned and discuss them with one another. By placing their posters throughout the school they will "testify" to their desire to create peace and harmony throughout the school and their belief that each person can help make it happen.

Description:

Students brainstorm ideas for slogans for posters that encourage everyone to contribute to creating a peaceful and harmonious school environment. The ideas are charted as they are generated. Next, the students engage in the process of creating their posters artistically. Finally, the posters are looked at one by one by the class and then posted on bulletin boards or hung from the ceilings of the classroom and school.

Objectives:

Students will:

— brainstorm creative slogans for posters encouraging everyone to contribute to making the classroom and school a peaceful and harmonious environment.

— create posters while sharing ideas for wordings and artistic presentations.

— post their posters.

Time needed:

One or two 40 to 60 minute class periods for brainstorming and making the posters. Additional time will be needed for posting the posters.

Materials needed:

Chalkboard or chart for charting ideas for posters; large colored sheets of construction paper for posters and available art materials. (Posters that are "collages" — torn paper in contrasting colors, cloth, ribbons and trim would be particularly eye-catching.) You may wish to enrich this activity by playing light instrumental background music while the students create.

Directions:

1. Introduce the activity: *Let's finish this unit by making posters with slogans and messages about how to create a peaceful and harmonious classroom and school. You don't have to be a great artist to make a colorful and interesting poster and you may work alone or with a partner.*

2. Suggest brainstorming: *Before we begin to use the art materials let's give each other some ideas for the slogans and messages we could write on the posters. Just let your mind loose and remember the points we've learned recently about creating peace and harmony. As you come up with ideas I'll*

write them down. Perhaps an idea someone else suggests will be just what you are looking for. If you want to take notes that's fine. It could help you decide how to word your slogan or message for your poster.

3. As needed, provide examples. Here are a few suggestions:

- Finish this sentence: (There are dozens of possibilities.) "Create peace and harmony by..."

- Ideas from "The principle of Unity and Diversity." For example: "If you look closely you can see yourself in everyone else." Or: "There's nobody else who's just like you — appreciate yourself!"

- Ideas from the fables and their morals. Many of the morals would work well. For example: "There are few things more beautiful than a kind heart!"

4. Give the students sufficient time to create their posters. Encourage them to discuss the wordings of their slogans and give each other artistic ideas while they work. Expect laughter and joking around.

5. After all of the posters have been completed look at them one by one as a class. Comment on at least one attractive element in each poster and encourage the students to compliment each other's results as well.

6. Assist the students to display their posters either on bulletin boards or hanging from the ceiling in the classroom and throughout the school.

GREAT RESOURCES

PUBLICATIONS

The resources listed below provided many ideas for this curriculum. They offer valuable information and suggestions for classroom activities, as well as guidelines and strategies to help schools prevent violence:

- *Aggressive and Violent Students* by Robert P. Bowman, Jo Lynn Johnson, Michael Paget and Mary Thomas-Williams, Chapin, South Carolina: Youth Light, Inc., 1998. Phone: (800) 209-9774.

- *As Tough As Necessary: Countering Violence, Aggression, and Hostility in Our Schools* by Richard L. Curwin and Allen N. Mendler, Alexandria, Virginia: Association for Supervision and Curriculum Development, 1997. Phone: (800) 933-2723.

- *Central High* an interactive movie on CD ROM, produced by Destiny Ineractive. Available from Compu-Teach Software Company. Phone: (800) 448-3224.

- *Character Education in America's Schools* by Terri Akin, M.S., Gerry Dunne, Ph.D., Susanna Palomares, M.A., and Dianne Schilling, M.S., Carson, California: Innerchoice Publishing Company, 1995. Phone: (310) 816-3085.

- *Conflict Resolution Skills for Teens* by David Cowan, M.A., Susanna Palomares, M.S., and Dianne Schilling, M.S., Carson, California: Innerchoice Publishing Company, 1994. Phone: (310) 816-3085.

- *Helping Teens Stop Violence: A Practical Guide for Counselors, Educators, and Parents* by Allen Creighton, Battered Women's Alternatives and Paul Kivel, Oakland Men's Project, Alameda, California: Hunter House, Inc., Publishers, 1992. Phone: (510) 865-5282.

- *Impact! A Self-Esteem Based Skill Development Program for Secondary Students* by Gerry Dunne, Ph.D., Dianne Schilling, M.S. and David Cowan, M.A., Carson, California: Innerchoice Publishing Company, 1990. Phone: (310) 816-3085.

- *Learning the Skills of Peacemaking: A K - 6 Activity Guide on Resolving Conflict, Communicating, Cooperating* by Naomi Drew, Carson, California: Jalmar Press, 1995. Phone: (310) 816-3085.

- *Managing Conflict: Strategies, Activities and Role Plays for Kids* by Susanna Palomares, M.A., and Terri Akin, M.S., Carson, California: Innerchoice Publishing Company, 1995. Phone: (310) 816-3085.

- *Peace Patrol: Creating a New Generation of Problem Solvers and Peacemakers* by Eden Steele, Carson, California: Innerchoice Publishing Company, 1994. Phone: (310) 816-3085.

- *Safe Schools, Safe Students: A Guide to Violence Prevention Strategies* by Drug Strategies, Washington, DC: 1998. Phone: (202) 663-6090.

- *Teaching the Skills of Conflict Resolution: Activities and Strategies for Counselors and Teachers* by David Cowan, M.A., Susanna Palomares, M.S., and Dianne Schilling, M.S., Carson, California: Innerchoice Publishing Company, 1992. Phone: (310) 816-3085.

- *The Close Call*, a booklet for students by Gerry Dunne, Ph.D., Torrance, California: Jalmar Press, 2001. Phone: (800) 662-9662.

- *Television and the Lives of Our Children: A Manual for Teachers and Parents* by Gloria DeGaetano, M.Ed., Redmond, Washington: Train of Thought Counseling, Publisher, 1993. Phone: (425) 883-1544

- *The Anger Workbook* by Lorrainne Bilodeau, M.S., Center City, Minnesota: Hazelden Educational Materials, 1992. Phone: (800) 328-9000.

- *The Coolien Challenge: Youth Violence Prevention* an interactive CD ROM produced by EDR Enterprises, 1998. Available from Compu-Teach Educational Software Company. Phone: (800) 448-3224.

- *The Peaceful Classroom in Action: A K - 6 Activity Guide on How to Create One and How to Keep It!* by Naomi Drew, Carson, California: Jalmar Press, 1999. Phone: (310) 816-3085.

- *The Moral Compass* by William J. Bennett, New York: Simon & Schuster, 1995.

- *What Kids Need to Succeed: Proven, Practical Ways to Raise Good Kids* by Peter L. Benson, Ph.D., Judy Galbraith, M.A., and Pamela Espeland, Minneapolis, Minnesota: Free Spirit Publishing, Inc., 1995. Phone: (612) 338-2068.

About the Author

Author, presenter, and teacher of teachers, Dr. Gerry Dunne began her career in education as a classroom teacher in the 1960s. Later, she developed a nationwide training system for teachers and school counselors to utilize curriculum she authored and published aimed at increasing emotional intelligence and prosocial skills in students from kindergarten through grade twelve.

For over 20 years, Gerry taught courses and conducted experiential workshops related to character education, child and adolescent growth and development, team building, conflict management, career development, stress management, self esteem, instructional design, parent education, effective teaching strategies and other topics related to education and human development. Many of her books and manuals have been translated into other languages including Spanish, French, Dutch and Hebrew.

Gerry has served as a university professor and education/training consultant to school districts, agencies and private organizations. She earned her B.A. degree at Chapman University, M.S. degree in Educational Administration at the University of Southern California and a Ph.D. degree in Psychology at the Saybrook Institute.

A recent honor: Gerry was selected "Alumnus of the Year," by the Chapman University Alumni Association.